Who is this Jesus?

A prophet? A great teacher? A lunatic?
... Or someone else?

Who is this Jesus?

A prophet? A great teacher? A lunatic?
... Or someone else?

E. M. Hicham

EP BOOKS
Faverdale North, Darlington, DL3 0PH, England

web: http://www.epbooks.org
e-mail: sales@epbooks.org

EP BOOKS USA
P. O. Box 614, Carlisle, PA 17013, USA

web: http://www.epbooks.us
e-mail: usasales@epbooks.org

First published 2010

British Library Cataloguing in Publication Data available

ISBN-13   978-0-85234-718-8   ISBN 0-85234-718-9

All Scripture quotations, unless otherwise indicated, are taken from the New King James Version. Copyright © 1979, 1980, 1982 by Thomas Nelson, Inc. Used by permission. All rights reserved.

Printed and bound in Great Britain by J F Print Ltd.

Acknowledgements

Many people have contributed to the writing of this book. So I express my profound appreciation to the following people, who assisted me in making this work far better than it would have been if I had not relied on them.

To my precious wife. It was such a joy to have her helping in this work. Her support to me through the process of its development was priceless. She has loved me and prayed for me much. Her comments on my book were of tremendous help. I owe a special debt of thanks to her for painstakingly editing my notes. Readers will never know how much clearer and smoother it is as a result.

Mike de Jong (my father-in-law), Paul Simpson, Jim Inman, Andy McIntosh, Peter Williams, Howard Crossley and Steve Taylor for kindly taking time to read my manuscript and making helpful comments and suggestions.

Above all, I give praise, honour and thanksgiving to the glorious sufficient Saviour Jesus Christ, of whom this book endeavours to speak. The more I study God's Holy Word (the Bible), the more astonished I am at the greatness and majesty that is his alone. My deepest desire is that he will be pleased with the efforts here. For all that acknowledges the deity of Christ, I gladly give God the glory; and for all that misses the mark, I pray for his forgiveness and correction. God alone is worthy, and so to him be all praise and worship, both now and for ever.

Contents

To
Jesus Christ

He is despised and rejected by men,
A Man of sorrows and acquainted with grief…

… we esteemed Him stricken,
Smitten by God, and afflicted.
But He was wounded for our transgressions,
He was bruised for our iniquities;
The chastisement for our peace was upon Him,
And by His stripes we are healed.
All we like sheep have gone astray;
We have turned, every one, to his own way;
And the LORD has laid on Him the iniquity of us all.

He was oppressed and He was afflicted,
Yet He opened not His mouth;
He was led as a lamb to the slaughter,
And as a sheep before its shearers is silent,
So He opened not His mouth…
For He was cut off from the land of the living;
For the transgressions of My people He was stricken.
And they made His grave with the wicked —
But with the rich at His death,
Because He had done no violence,
Nor was any deceit in His mouth.

Yet it pleased the LORD to bruise Him;
He has put Him to grief

(Isaiah, chapter 53, verses 3-10).

Foreword

Without doubt the key figure of human history is Jesus Christ. If you live in the western world the date written on the coins in your pocket and on today's newspaper has been fixed with reference to his birth. Jesus Christ never wrote a book or song yet more books and songs have been written about him than about any other person who has ever lived.

Jesus Christ never took up a sword, nor led an army, yet all of the armies who have ever marched have not affected history as much as he has. His teachings are unsurpassed, his miracles are unique, and he lived without sin of any kind. Three days after his death his tomb was empty and hundreds of his followers claimed that he conquered death itself.

Today, he has followers in every country of the world. Over two billion people claim allegiance to him. So who is he? This excellent book by E. M. Hicham seeks to answer that important question by considering the writings of the prophets, the words of eyewitnesses and by examining what Jesus himself said. I strongly recommend this book and urge you to read it thoughtfully so that you may answer for yourself that vital question: 'Who is this Jesus?'

Dr Steve Taylor,
Reader in Electrical Engineering and Electronics,
University of Liverpool, England,
and Chairman of United Beach Missions, UK and Europe
May 2010

Introduction

'What's so special about your Jesus? Why do you tell people to trust him to the exclusion of any other saviour?' Big question — and a valid one.

Christianity is Christ. All that Christians hold dear is centred on Jesus Christ. If you take Jesus out of the picture, Christianity becomes an empty shell.

What do you think of Jesus?

The opinions about Jesus are countless in seemingly every area of culture. Some people do not reject all of Jesus' work on earth, though they do reject his claim to deity. They say that Jesus was merely a good man to be respected solely for his teaching, love, justice and healing; but they are not clear about his being the God-Man. He was sent to earth as a great moral teacher rather than as a mediator.

Those who embrace atheism have a low view of Jesus. He is less than most people think he is. Bertrand Russell, a famous apologist of the atheistic viewpoint, said, 'I cannot myself feel that either in the matter of wisdom or in the matter of virtue Christ stands quite as high as some other people known to history.'[1]

Mormons teach that Jesus was a pre-existent spirit who became one of many gods; furthermore, they teach that he was a polygamist and a half-brother of Lucifer. The Jehovah's Witnesses' opinion is that Jesus is a created being who was given the status of second-in-command. To them Jesus is 'a god, but not the Almighty God, who is Jehovah'.[2] Instead, they say that Jesus is 'a created individual' who 'is the second greatest personage of the universe'.[3] New Age guru Deepak Chopra said, 'I see Christ as a state of consciousness we can all aspire to.'[4] Sun Myung Moon teaches that Jesus' value is no greater than that of any other man. Those who follow Moon's teaching say that Jesus' work was a failure. Muslims believe that Jesus 'was only a messenger of Allah' (Qur'an, Surah 4:171). They also say he was a sinless prophet who never achieved the greatness of the prophet Muhammad. Buddhism teaches that Jesus was not God but rather an enlightened man like the Buddha. Hinduism, with its many views of Jesus, does not consider him to be the only God, but most likely a wise man or incarnation of God much like Krishna. The Dalai Lama said, '[Jesus] was either a fully enlightened being, or a bodhisvatta [a being who aids others to enlightenment] of a very high spiritual realization.'[5] Indian Hindu leader Mahatma Gandhi said, 'I cannot ascribe exclusive divinity to Jesus. He is as divine as Krishna or Rama or Muhammad or Zoroaster.'[6]

Fidel Castro said, 'I never saw a contradiction between the ideas that sustain me and the ideas of that symbol, of that extraordinary figure [Jesus Christ].'[7] Mikhail Gorbachev said, 'Jesus was the first socialist, the first to seek a better life for mankind.'[8] There is even a Canadian nudist-arsonist cult that thinks that the word 'Jesus' in the Bible is a code word for hallucinogenic mushrooms that are to be eaten before stripping off their clothes and setting things on fire.

So which of the mentioned opinions about Jesus is yours? When Jesus asked his disciples what people thought about him, they answered, 'Some say John the Baptist, some Elijah, and others Jeremiah or one of the prophets.' It was obvious to people who lived during Jesus' time on earth that he was a prophet. But Jesus insisted, 'Who do you say that I am?' The apostle Peter answered, 'You are the Christ, the Son of the Living God' (Bible, Matthew 16:14-16).

What a statement! In other words, Peter said, 'People say you are a prophet, but I say that you are more than a prophet; you are the Son of God.' True Christians, like the apostle Peter, believe that Jesus is actually fully human and fully divine at the same time.

One thing is for sure. Somebody is wrong! These people cannot all be right about Jesus. He cannot be exactly who all these people say he is. Many people who think they know, do not know in reality. If he is only a prophet or medium, then those who insist he is God are wrong. If

on the other hand he is God, then those who insist that
he is only an exceptional man are wrong. In science and
investigative journalism, we pursue truth passionately.
Why should it be different in this important realm?

People often ask where the Bible says that Jesus claimed
to be God. Suppose a man approached you and said, 'I
am God, worship me.' Would you believe him, let alone
worship him? Of course not! You would think he was a
self-centred idiot, a blasphemer or a lunatic. It would be
like someone saying, 'I'm a walnut.' We would say, 'No,
you're just nuts!'

Jesus knew how people would respond if he claimed to
be God in such a foolish way. Instead, he demonstrated
his identity in numerous indirect, but clear ways. Jesus'
opponents certainly understood what he meant. In fact,
they tried to kill him because of it.

What matters in the end is not how Jesus made the
claim, but whether there is clear evidence that he is indeed
God. If we can find proof of his divine identity, then we
must worship him. Do you wish to understand the biblical
faith? Then please consider the evidence contained in this
book honestly and with an open mind. The Christian faith
rests on facts. We will examine them together and decide
whether Jesus really is God.

1.

What did the prophets say about Jesus?

Hundreds of years before Jesus was born, God sent messengers to tell us about a Saviour who would come to deal with mankind's greatest problem. God gradually made his great plan of salvation known to the Hebrew people, so that, through them, all nations would be blessed. Prophets were sent to warn and teach many different generations, but their words centred on one great theme: the Messiah Saviour and what he would do. The Messiah (chosen one) would save people from the power and punishment of sin in order that they might know God and have a relationship with him. In his own teaching Jesus Christ spoke of these prophets and confirmed that they foresaw both his coming and his identity.

We could look at numerous statements of the prophets which show that they were longing for the coming of the great Messiah. Here we will consider just a few examples.

The prophet David (*ca* 1000 B.C.)

David was a great king of Israel who lived about a thousand years before Jesus. He prophesied many times about the coming Messiah in the Psalms. In each prophecy, the Messiah is referred to as God himself.

In Psalm 45, for example, David says of the Messiah, 'Your throne, O God, is forever and ever.' In another psalm about the Messiah, David writes, 'You laid the foundation of the earth, and the heavens are the work of Your hands.' The Messiah is also the Creator. He continues: 'But You are the same, and Your years will have no end' (Bible, Psalm 102:25-27). The Messiah is eternal. Again, in Psalm 110:1 the Messiah is called 'Lord', and is said to be ruling on the throne of God.

The writer of one of the New Testament letters, called Hebrews, quotes each of these psalms and applies them directly to Jesus Christ (Bible, Hebrews 1:5-13).

The prophet Isaiah (*ca* 700 B.C.)

Seven hundred years before the birth of Jesus, a prophet called Isaiah talked about the Messiah's life and identity in amazing detail. About his birth, he wrote, 'The virgin shall conceive and bear a Son, and shall call his name Immanuel [which means God-With-Us]' (Bible, Isaiah 7:14; see also Matthew 1:23). The child would be born of a woman, but his birth would be of divine origin.

A few pages later, Isaiah continues: 'Unto us a Child is born, unto us a Son is given; and the government will be upon His shoulder. And His name will be called Wonderful, Counsellor, Mighty God, Everlasting Father, Prince of Peace' (Bible, Isaiah 9:6). Let us unpack this prophecy. The Son who was to come would be called:

Wonderful. This word is generally used in Hebrew to describe miraculous works of God. A miracle is something that is beyond the scope of human ability. In other words, it is something only God can do.

Counsellor. His every instruction is wonderful. His opinions are extraordinary. His recommendations are impressive. His advice is phenomenal. He is the only one worth listening to. Jesus is the wisdom of God. The promised Son would do things that only God can do. Just in case we are in any doubt, Isaiah tells us that God himself is 'wonderful in counsel and excellent in guidance' (Bible, Isaiah 28:29).

Mighty God. The child would be both divine and powerful. Jehovah (God) is referred to as 'Mighty God' in Isaiah 10:20-21 and Jeremiah 32:18. In our text, Isaiah applies the same Hebrew word to the Son (Jesus) who would be born!

Everlasting Father. This literally means 'Father of eternity'. The rule of the promised Messiah knows no end. His government is like that of a father. In Jesus Christ we have a love that will not let us go.

Prince of Peace. Jesus is the exclusive owner of peace. He said, 'Peace I leave with you, My peace I give to you; not as the world gives do I give to you' (Bible, John 14:27). The peace that Jesus gives is divine. Jesus offers peace to men and women through faith in him.

Seven hundred years after this prophecy was given, an angel appeared to a young woman called Mary who lived in the town of Nazareth. The angel brought a wonderful message. She was told that she would be the mother of Jesus, the Saviour. 'He will be great, and will be called the Son of the Highest... And He will reign over the house of Jacob for ever, and of His kingdom there will be no end.' Understandably, Mary was puzzled, since she was a virgin. The angel replied, 'The Holy Spirit will come upon you, and the power of the Highest will overshadow you; therefore, also, that Holy One who is to be born will be called the Son of God' (Bible, Luke 1:30-35).

> The prophet Isaiah proclaimed that the child [Jesus] ... would be human, yes, but a child who was also divine.

Long before a baby cried in a manger in Bethlehem, the prophet Isaiah proclaimed that this child would be unique. A human child, yes, but a child who was also divine.

The prophet Micah (*ca* 700 B.C.)

The prophet Micah foretold that the Messiah would be born in 'Bethlehem Ephrathah'. Though it was a small, insignificant town, the one born there would be 'Ruler in Israel, whose goings forth are from of old, from everlasting' (Bible, Micah 5:2). Micah revealed that the Messiah to be born in Bethlehem many years later was actually already in existence. In fact, he had always existed. Who is eternal except God?

The prophet John the Baptist (*ca* A.D. 30)

Before Jesus began his public ministry, John the Baptist had been preaching in the desert for some time, calling people to turn back to God in preparation for the arrival of someone far greater. John claimed to have come in fulfilment of a prophecy made by Isaiah, 'The voice of one crying in the wilderness: "Prepare the way of the LORD; make straight in the desert a highway *for our God*"' (Bible, Isaiah 40:3). John clearly considered Jesus to be Jehovah, God himself, spoken of in Isaiah 40:3.

Can we trust the prophecies?

You may say, 'That's all very well, but how do we know that these prophecies were written hundreds of years before Jesus was born? What if they were simply written afterwards to make Jesus look special?' It is not hard to prove that the prophecies are genuine. To do so, we must simply look at the Scriptures that the Jews cherish to this day. The Jewish Scriptures are identical to the first part of the Christian Bible.

You may know that the Bible is divided into two sections, commonly called the Old Testament (written before the birth of Christ) and the New Testament (written after the birth of Jesus). The prophecies mentioned above are found in the Old Testament, which has been strictly guarded by the Jews over the centuries. They would never have allowed them to be altered. If anyone had tried to add the above prophecies, there would have been a public outcry. History records no such occurrence. Furthermore, the Jews are the last people who would want to add anything about Jesus to their Scriptures. Remember, most of them hated him. They were waiting for the Messiah, but they wanted a great political leader who would deliver them from Roman domination, forgetting that their own Scriptures promised a Messiah who would sacrifice himself to save them from the power of sin. They did not like that. So why would they allow anyone to add prophecies about a coming Saviour who would do the very things they did not want?

Alex, a friend of mine, is Jewish. He told me that during all his visits to the synagogue, he never once heard a rabbi reading Isaiah 53, which details the Messiah's life and what he would experience on the cross. When Alex heard about the prophecies, he compared them with the record of the life of Jesus in the New Testament, and was amazed at what he discovered. For the first time he realized that Jesus must be the one mentioned in the Jewish Scriptures. He has been a follower of Jesus ever since.

We can know with confidence that the prophecies are genuine. Many more examples could be given of promises about the Messiah's identity, but surely from those we have considered, it is clear that the prophets of the Old Testament knew that the promised Saviour would be God himself.

2.

What did the apostles say about Jesus?

To start with, what is an apostle? The Greek word *apostolos* means 'one sent forth', an ambassador. The biblical apostles were men chosen by Jesus (Bible, Luke 6:13) and sent out by him. They travelled with him. They saw his miracles. They heard him teaching during the last three years of his life and after his resurrection. Their legacy is the benchmark by which all Christian teaching should be judged. These men knew Jesus better than anyone else, and they believed that he was God. They held fast to that truth whatever the cost. In fact, most of the apostles were tortured and killed in later years because they would not deny their faith in Jesus Christ. Here is what three of these apostles wrote about him.

The apostle John

John's Gospel chapter 1

You may know that the New Testament part of the Bible contains four accounts of the life of Jesus, which are known as 'Gospels'. 'Gospel' simply means 'good news'. One of these accounts was written by the apostle John.

The Bible often refers to Jesus as 'The Word of God' (see Revelation 19:13, for example). Our words express who we are. In a similar way, Jesus the Word of God is the tangible expression of who God is. John's Gospel begins, 'In the beginning was the Word, and the Word was with God, and *the Word was God*... All things were made through him and without him nothing was made that was made' (Bible, John 1:1, 3).

What can we learn about the Word from this text?

- The Word was 'in the beginning'. The Word pre-existed the creation of the world.
- The Word was active in creation. He created everything in the universe.
- The Word was with God.
- The Word was God. Here we find a clear assertion of the deity of Christ.

We are even more amazed as we read on and see that the Word, who is God, 'became flesh and dwelt among us, and we beheld His glory, the glory as of the only begotten of the Father, full of grace and truth' (Bible, John 1:14). God himself came to earth in the form of a man so that we could know what he is like.

> God himself came to earth in the form of a man so that we could know what he is like.

The Mormons and 'Jehovah's Witnesses'

Mormons and 'Jehovah's Witnesses' (JWs) perform incredible linguistic gymnastics in order to evade the plain teaching of this text. Indeed they torture the passage to wrestle their views out of it!

Until around 1950, JWs carried with them a copy of the American Standard Version of the Bible (because God's name is translated as Jehovah throughout the Old Testament). But they faced the embarrassing problem of trying to deny the deity of Christ, while their Bible said plainly that 'the Word is God'. So the Watchtower Society published its own New World Translation of the Holy Scripture, produced by a five-man 'Translation Committee': N. H. Knorr, F. W. Franz, A. D. Schroeder, G. D. Grangas and M. Henschel.

These men had no adequate schooling or background in Bible translation. Apart from Franz, *none* of the committee members knew biblical Greek or Hebrew, and even Franz's ability is open to serious question. Franz's 'expertise' in the biblical languages amounted to a mere two years of Greek at a university and he was self-taught in Hebrew. Yet he was regarded as the Society's best translator!

Without sufficient knowledge of the original languages, men like Franz were clearly not qualified to translate the Scriptures. They invented their own rules of Greek grammar and then applied those rules only in places where they were needed to support their peculiar theology. A clear example of this is John 1:1 where the New World

Translation (NWT) renders the Greek '*and the Word was a god*'.

Is the Word 'a god'?

The Witnesses use flawed linguistic arguments to justify their translation of this verse. In the original text the definite article *the* is not there. Greek has no indefinite article, *a*. Normally, when a noun appears without *the*, the indefinite article *a* may be supplied *only if the context warrants it*. If ever a context prohibited such an insertion, it is the context of this verse. If Mormons and JWs insert the indefinite article *a* here, they slip into polytheism. If the Word is *a* god, but not *the* God, we must ask: How many gods are there? If we know anything about the author of John's Gospel, we know that he was a monotheist.

As a matter of fact, JWs are inconsistent in their argument. In the very chapter in which John 1:1 is found, the word 'God' occurs at least four other times without the definite article, and yet in each instance it is rendered God, not *a god*. In John 1:6 we read, in the NWT, 'There arose a man that was sent forth as a representative of God; his name is John.' Since the Greek has no definite article, the Witnesses, to be consistent with their grammatical rule, ought to translate it: 'sent from a god'. Verses 12 and 13 are translated 'God's children', and 'born of God'. Why not 'children of a god', and 'born of a god'? In the eighteenth verse we read, 'No man has seen God at any time.' Why do the Witnesses not translate it, 'No man has seen a god at any time'? This makes it clear that Jehovah's Witnesses do not really believe their own rule of translation. We must conclude that they translate John 1:1 as they do, not on the basis of careful grammatical study of the Bible, but on the basis of their presupposition that Jesus is not God.

There is one more interesting thing to note. The JW New World Translation still calls Jesus 'God' in John 20:28 and Isaiah 9:6! In fact their 1985 *Kingdom interlinear* version reveals that the Greek literally says Jesus is 'the God' where the apostle Thomas called Jesus, 'My Lord and My God' (Bible, John 20:28).

Jesus is the Word through whom all things were made. There is no doubt that the apostle John identified Jesus as the Creator God.

1 John 5:20

In addition to his account of the life of Jesus, the apostle John wrote three letters to Christians which are found in the Bible. He also wrote the last book of the Bible, Revelation.

John concludes his first letter: 'We know that the Son of God has come and has given us an understanding, that we may know Him who is true; and we are in Him who is true, in *His Son Jesus Christ. This is the true God and eternal life*' (Bible, 1 John 5:19-20).

What clearer words could be used to teach that Jesus is God!

The apostle Peter

As one of the original twelve disciples, the apostle Peter gained firsthand insight into the character and work of his Lord Jesus. He once said to Jesus, '…You know all things, and have no need that anyone should question You. By this we believe that You came forth from God' (Bible, John 16:30).

Peter did not just see Jesus' public miracles; he was also among the inner circle of disciples. At one time they witnessed Jesus being transformed so that 'His face shone like the sun, and His clothes became as white as the light.' Peter heard God the Father calling Jesus his 'beloved Son' (Bible, Matthew 17:2-6). Jesus appeared to Peter several times after his resurrection, when he was on his own and when he was accompanied by others. He watched as Jesus was taken up to heaven. So we should not be surprised to find Peter speaking of the divinity of Jesus Christ.

2 Peter 1:1

In his second letter, the apostle Peter opens with the words, 'Simon Peter, a bondservant and apostle of Jesus Christ, to those who have obtained like precious faith with us by the righteousness of *our God and Saviour Jesus Christ*' (Bible, 2 Peter 1:1).

Greek scholars affirm that the original language is constructed with only one article ('the') before this phrase, so the entire phrase refers to the same person. Peter identifies Jesus Christ as both Saviour and God!

The apostle Paul

Romans 9:5

The apostle Paul wrote, '*Christ came, who is over all, the eternally blessed God.* Amen' (Bible, Romans 9:5).

The punctuation of the Greek text has been debated, but the overwhelming majority of evidence indicates that we have in this verse not an independent declaration about God ('God blessed for ever'), but a statement praising Christ in his deity.

Titus 2:13

Writing to a fellow pastor called Titus, Paul clearly wrote that Jesus is God. He told Christians to look 'for the blessed hope and glorious appearing of *our great God and Saviour Jesus Christ*' (Bible, Titus 2:13). This is a clear reference to the deity of Jesus.

Colossians 1:15-20

Writing to a church in Colosse (modern Turkey), the apostle Paul wrote a statement which reveals that Jesus has a unique status.

'He [Jesus] is the image of the invisible God...' If we want to know what God is like, we must look at Jesus. God cannot be seen, but in Jesus he revealed himself in a way that we could understand.

'...the firstborn over all creation...' In using the word 'firstborn', the apostle Paul is not telling us that Jesus Christ was the first thing to be born. That is not what the word 'firstborn' means in the Old Testament. Solomon was certainly not the first of King David's sons, yet he was named the firstborn (Bible, Psalm 89:27). The people of Israel as a whole were sometimes called 'firstborn' to indicate their high position as recipients of God's love (Bible, Exodus 4:22; Jeremiah 31:9). The word 'firstborn' means that Jesus has a unique status. He has the highest position, the superior place, the pre-eminence. That is what the word 'firstborn' means. Wherever you go, Jesus enjoys the first place. No one is in a more senior position. Why?

'...For by Him all things were created that are in heaven and that are on earth, visible and invisible, whether thrones or

dominions or principalities or powers. All things were created through Him and for Him.' Jesus has the highest place of honour because he is the Creator of the universe. And not just the Creator…

'…And He is before all things, and in Him all things consist…' He sustains the universe and holds it together.

'…For it pleased the Father that in Him all the fulness should dwell…' Let me explain the word 'fulness'. Imagine you are taking a coach journey in a vehicle that can hold fifty-six passengers. The driver stands at the door checking and counting the passengers' tickets as they climb on. When fifty-six have been counted he says, 'The coach is full. There are no more people to come.' That is the meaning of the Greek word 'fulness'. No more to come! Christ is so fully God that there is no more Godhood to come. The Lord Jesus Christ is God in exactly the same sense, exactly the same way, as the Father is God. From head to toe he is God. There is not one speck or detail of deity missing. That is why he is able to do what no mere man could ever do: save us from the power and consequences of sin and restore our relationship with God.

'…and by Him to reconcile all things to Himself, by Him, whether things on earth or things in heaven, having made peace through the blood of His cross' (Bible, Colossians 1:15-20). God is angry with me. Left to myself I will never have

peace with God, because by nature I am separated from him. The wrong things I have thought, said and done alienate me from God. I am cursed because I have broken God's law. BUT, Jesus Christ became a curse for me. He took the curse on himself so that I would be free from it. On the cross, Jesus suffered the punishment that I deserve for my wrongdoing. That is the basis of my peace with God. If Jesus was just a man, he could not have healed the relationship between God and Man. The only arbitrator or mediator who could bring God and Man together was one who was both God *and* Man. A few paragraphs later Paul wrote, *'In Him [Christ] dwells all the fulness of the Godhead bodily'* (Bible, Colossians 2:9).

Philippians 2:5-11

Writing to another church, Paul said, 'Let this mind be in you which was also in Christ Jesus, who, *being in the form of God, did not consider it robbery to be equal with God,* but made Himself of no reputation, taking the form of a bondservant, and coming in the likeness of men' (Bible, Philippians 2:5-7).

What is Paul saying here?

Imagine that you are watching television one Thursday. Suddenly, the front door opens and two men walk into the room, say 'Good evening,' walk over to the TV, pull out the aerial, disconnect the DVD player, pick up the

TV and walk out. You say, 'Good night', and they reply, 'Good night'. Why isn't it robbery? I'll tell you. Your own TV is broken, so you have borrowed another one for two weeks. The people you borrowed it from said that they would come to collect it on Thursday. So when they took the TV you did not think that it was robbery because it was already theirs.

> Jesus did not think that having equality with God was robbery because it was already his!

Jesus did not think that having equality with God was robbery because it was already his! He was God in his own right.

Later Paul continues by stating that when Jesus returns (because he will!), 'every knee should bow, of those in heaven, and of those on earth, and of those under the earth, and *that* every tongue should confess that Jesus Christ *is* Lord' (Bible, Philippians 2:10-11).

What Paul is saying here is that when Jesus comes back the whole universe, without exception, will worship him; even demons and people who have rejected Jesus as the Saviour. Angels and those who have trusted Jesus for salvation will do this joyfully. Demons and people who have rejected Jesus will do it ruefully and remorsefully (but not penitently). So great will Jesus' glory be that they will all feel impelled to confess, acknowledge and affirm that he is Lord.

This is a remarkable thing to say of Jesus at his return! Why? Because this response to Jesus is identical to the Old Testament description of the way people would respond to God Jehovah. In other words, what is said of Jesus here can only be said of God. Let me explain. Seven hundred years before the birth of Jesus, God said through the prophet Isaiah, 'Look to Me, and be saved, all you ends of the earth! For I am God, and there is no other. I have sworn by Myself; the word has gone out of My mouth in righteousness, and shall not return, that *to Me every knee shall bow, every tongue shall take an oath*'[1] (Bible, Isaiah 45:22-23). Yet Paul takes these words and relates them to the coming universal acknowledgement that Jesus is Lord, demonstrating that Jesus is none other than God himself.

Furthermore, the name *'Lord'* is the New Testament synonym (equivalent) of the special name of God that is used in the Old Testament. The Old Testament was written in Hebrew. God's special name is written YHWH. Nobody knows how to pronounce it now. In English we often say 'Jehovah'. The day came when most Hebrew people could no longer read their own language. They could read Greek, however, so seventy Jewish men translated the Old Testament into Greek. When they came to YHWH, they used the word *Kurios* (Lord). When Paul wrote this letter to the Philippians he said, 'That at the name of Jesus every knee should bow, of those in heaven, and under the earth, and that every tongue should confess that Jesus Christ is *Kurios!*'

Say *Kurios* to a Greek-speaking reader of the Old
Testament and he or she will immediately think of the
holy name of God, YHWH. Jesus has the same name
because he is God in his own right.

Loyalty of early Christians

One of the great crises that faced the early Christian
community was its relationship to the civil authorities,
particularly the Roman government. Nero had established
an emperor-worship cult. We read in church history of the
persecution and martyrdom of many Christians under his
rule. As an oath of loyalty, Nero made every citizen in the
Roman Empire recite a brief formula: *Kaisar kurios*, which
means, 'Caesar is lord.'

The Christians' response was, 'We will honour the
civil magistrates; we will pay our tithes and our tributes
to Caesar. We will do all we can to be model citizens of
Rome. But one thing we cannot say, privately or publicly,
are those two words: *Kaisar kurios*, because to do so would
be to commit cosmic treason, because our Lord, our *kurios*,
is Christ Jesus.'

Consequently, by order of Nero, the Christians were
coated in pitch and set on fire, to become human torches
to illuminate Nero's gardens at night. Other Christians
had to face lions in the arena of the Circus Maximus.

One Christian man called Polycarp,[2] at the age of
eighty-six, was charged with treason because he refused

to recite the oath to Caesar. Because he was respected and venerable, the prosecutors did not want to harm him. They brought him into the arena before thousands of spectators, but even up to the last moments the state officials wanted to spare him from execution. They gave him one last opportunity. All Polycarp needed to say was, 'Caesar is lord', and, 'Away with the atheists!' (It is one of the ironies of history that the Christians were charged with atheism because they wouldn't worship the emperor.)

Polycarp calmly smiled and said, 'If that's all you want me to say, I can say that.' He looked at the stands, where the representatives of the Roman state and the pagan religions were seated, and said, 'Away with the atheists!' His opinion of who the 'atheists' were clearly differed from theirs! And then Polycarp said, 'Eighty-six years have I been faithful to my Lord (Jesus), and for eighty-six years He has been merciful and gracious to me. How can I now deny Him? *Iesus ho kurios* (Jesus is Lord).' He was immediately executed.

Polycarp is just one example of many who, like most of the apostles, gave their lives because they loved Jesus and believed that he was God.

3.

What did Jesus say about himself?

The prophets foretold that the promised Saviour would be both human and divine. The apostles clearly testified that Jesus Christ was God. If we stop at this point, this may be enough to convince us of the deity of Jesus. But there is more. We need to look at what Jesus believed about himself.

In the Scriptures, the names of God are given to Jesus Christ. We have already mentioned some of them like *Immanuel* (which means 'God with us'), and *Lord* (Kurios) and considered their significance. There are other divine names and titles which Jesus applied to himself.

'I am'

One of Jesus' most famous claims is found in John 8:58. He said to the Jews, 'Most assuredly, I say to you, before Abraham was, *I AM*.' This was an incredible statement! Consider the following facts:

- Abraham lived more than two thousand years before Jesus, yet Jesus was claiming to have existed before Abraham. He was claiming to be eternal. But that was not all.

- When God revealed himself to Moses, the great leader of Israel, he said, 'I AM WHO I AM' (Bible, Exodus 3:14). By using the expression, 'I AM', Jesus was actually using God's special name, YHWH. He was claiming to be God. The people picked up stones and threw them at Jesus because they knew what he was saying.

Jesus clearly meant us to understand that he is God, who has come among us as a Man. What else could he mean when he prayed in the presence of his disciples, 'And now, O Father, glorify Me together with Yourself, with the glory which I had with You before the world was' (Bible, John 17:5).

The Bible calls God 'the eternal God' (Bible, Deuteronomy 33:27) who is 'from everlasting to everlasting' (Bible, Psalm 90:2). 'Jehovah-God' is called the 'first' and 'last' (Bible, Isaiah 44:6 and 48:12). In the book of Revelation, God says, 'I am the Alpha and the Omega, the Beginning and the End' (Revelation 21:6). Alpha and Omega are the first and last letters of the Greek alphabet. Yet in the same book Jesus says of himself, 'I am the Alpha and Omega ... who is and who was and who is to come, the Almighty' (Bible, Revelation 1:8). A few verses later, Jesus says, 'I am the First and the Last' (Bible, Revelation 1:17). Again at the end of the book, he says, 'I am the Alpha and the Omega, the Beginning and the End, the First and the Last' (Bible, Revelation 22:13). How can this be since there can be only one first and last? Only one beginning and end? Is this not conclusive evidence that Christ is 'Jehovah-Jesus'?

'The Son of Man'

The title, 'the Son of Man', is used about eighty times in the Bible. Jesus used this title for himself more than any other. Many people think it is just a reference to his humanity; his identification with us as people. There is an element of truth in this answer, but it is incomplete. 'Son of Man' is also a divine title.

The name, 'the Son of Man', was not invented by Jesus in the first century. It is rooted in the Old Testament, particularly in the book of the prophet Daniel which was written about six hundred years before Christ. The book of Daniel contains apocalyptic literature with vivid imagery.

In the seventh chapter, Daniel describes a vision of the interior of heaven itself. He uses sharp imagery to describe his experience:

'I watched till thrones were put in place,
And the Ancient of Days was seated;

His garment was white as snow,
And the hair of His head was like pure wool.
His throne was a fiery flame,
Its wheels a burning fire;
A fiery stream issued
And came forth from before Him.
A thousand thousands ministered to Him;
Ten thousand times ten thousand stood before Him.
The court was seated,
And the books were opened'

(Bible, Daniel 7:9-10).

Do you get the picture? Daniel, looking into the inner court of heaven, sees someone seated on a throne who has the title, 'the Ancient of Days'. He is referring to God the Father, seated in regal splendour, surrounded and attended by tens of thousands of angelic beings. The scene portrayed is that of a courtroom, where, with the Judge seated, the court comes to order, and the books are opened. We can imagine how breathtaking this was for the prophet: to see the future when God the King will judge us all.

But Daniel kept looking, and this is what he saw:

'I was watching in the night visions,
And behold, One like *the Son of Man,*
Coming with the clouds of heaven!
He came to the Ancient of Days,
And they brought Him near before Him.
Then to Him was given dominion

> and glory and a kingdom
> That all peoples, nations, and
>   languages should serve Him.
> His dominion is an everlasting dominion,
> Which shall not pass away,
> And His kingdom the one
> Which shall not be destroyed'
>   (Bible, Daniel 7:13-14).

Daniel is saying, 'I looked into heaven itself. Suddenly I saw the visible and tangible manifestation of the blinding glory of God displayed in the clouds. And in these clouds, being brought in to the throne room, was one who was identified as the Son of Man. He was presented to the Ancient of Days. The Ancient of Days then commanded that the Son of Man be given power and glory and an everlasting kingdom.' What Daniel saw was the exaltation of Jesus Christ.

The title 'Son of Man' is used, not to describe a human being whose sphere of operation is the earth, but to describe a heavenly being. It concerns one who left the presence of the Ancient of Days (God the Father) in heaven, became human, and at the completion of his work returned to his place of origin, heaven itself, where he was given dominion and glory.

So the title 'the Son of Man' is a divine title applied to the Messiah who exercises universal and eternal dominion. When Jesus used the title for himself, he was saying, 'I am that Son of Man.'

Jesus once said: 'No one has ascended to heaven but he who came down from heaven, that is, the Son of Man who is in heaven' (John 3:13). He often made reference to the fact that his place of origin was not Bethlehem. Yes, he was born in Bethlehem, but he predated his own birth. He repeatedly stressed the fact that he came from above, from the Father. He descended from heaven before he ever ascended to heaven.

It is no accident that when Jesus left this world after his resurrection, he ascended in a cloud of glory which disappeared beyond the vision of the disciples (Bible, Acts 1:9). Luke, the author of the book of Acts, tells us of Jesus' departure, but he does not describe his arrival at the other end. The arrival had already been described by the prophet Daniel years before it happened!

'The Son of God'

Jesus also called himself 'the Son of God' many times. He never once denied the title when other people gave it to him. He certainly would have done so if they had been mistaken. We have already seen that in many places Jesus spoke of God as 'My Father'.

The title Son of God does *not* mean that God had a wife. It does *not* mean that God married Mary who gave birth to Jesus. That would be blasphemous. The meaning is far deeper. The prophets like Abraham, Isaac, Moses, David and Isaiah would have understood the true meaning of 'Son of God'. We have already seen that the prophet Isaiah said that the Son, the Messiah, would be called, 'Wonderful, Counsellor, *Mighty God*, everlasting Father, and Prince of Peace' (Bible, Isaiah 9:6). If you asked any Jewish person before the birth of Jesus, 'Who can be called the Son of God?', he or she would reply, 'Only someone who is divine — equal to God.' That is why, when Jesus claimed to be the Son of God, they accused him of blasphemy and crucified him.

The sister of a man called Lazarus whom Jesus raised from the dead said, 'Yes, Lord, I believe that *You are the Christ, the Son of God*, who is to come into the world' (Bible, John 11:27). These were not new concepts to them but had been spoken of by the prophets for centuries. They had been waiting for him.

We mentioned in the introduction that the apostle Peter said to Jesus, 'You are the Christ, *the Son of the living God*.' Jesus called Peter 'blessed', saying, 'flesh and blood has not revealed this to you, but *My Father* who is in heaven' (Bible, Matthew 16:15-17).

When Jesus was arrested and brought before the Sanhedrin (the Jews' top political and religious tribunal), Caiaphas asked him the straightforward question: 'I put You under oath by the living God: *Tell us if you are the Christ, the Son of God!*' Without any hesitation Jesus replied, '*It is as you said*' (Bible, Matthew 26:63-64).

The next day Jesus was hauled before the Sanhedrin again, but nothing could make him change his mind. All of their interrogation came down to one question,

'*Are You then the Son of God?*' Jesus replied, '*You rightly say that I am*' (Bible, Luke 22:70). The authorities were furious and wanted to kill him. In both meetings they accused him of blaspheming. 'He has spoken blasphemy! What further need do we have of witnesses? Look, now you have heard His blasphemy!' (Bible, Matthew 26:65). Their question to Jesus was not, 'Are you one of the children of God?' If it was, Jesus' answer could not have occasioned a charge of blasphemy. The Jews clearly understood what Jesus meant by calling himself the Son of God. The eternal Son of God is God himself.

> The Jews clearly understood what Jesus meant by calling himself the Son of God. The eternal Son of God is God himself.

On other occasions Jesus emphasized his unity with God the Father. The Jews once asked Jesus, 'If you are the Christ, tell us plainly.' Jesus replied, 'I told you, and you do not believe… *I and My Father are one.*' What was the Jews' reaction to that? We read, 'Then the Jews took up stones again to stone Him.' When Jesus asked them why they behaved in this way, they said, 'For a good work we do not stone You, but for blasphemy, and because *You, being a Man, make Yourself God.*' Jesus then quoted from Psalm 82, reasoning that since the Israelites were called 'children of the Most High', how could they 'say of Him whom the Father sanctified and sent into the world, "You are blaspheming," because I said, "*I am the Son of God*"?' (Bible, John 10:22-36).

On one occasion Jesus healed a man on the Sabbath day (the weekly Jewish day of rest) and because of that the Jews tried to kill him. Jesus answered them, '*My Father* has been working until now, and I have been working' (Bible, John 5:17). The Jews understood what Jesus meant. They 'sought all the more to kill Him [Jesus], because He not only broke the Sabbath, but also said that God was His Father, *making Himself equal with God*' (Bible, John 5:18).

In John 1:18, we read, 'No one has seen God at any time. The only begotten Son, who is in the bosom of the Father, He has declared Him.' Nobody has ever seen God the Father except the Son. And yet to see Jesus is to see God, for he declares God perfectly. Philip, one of Jesus' disciples, once asked Jesus, 'Lord, show us the Father, and it is sufficient for us.' Jesus said to him, 'Have I been with you so long, and yet you have not known Me, Philip? *He who has seen Me has seen the Father*; so how can you say, "Show us the Father"? Do you not believe that *I am in the Father and the Father in Me*?' (Bible, John 14:1-11). Once again, when the Jewish people heard this, they persecuted Jesus and tried to kill him because by claiming his equality with the Father, Jesus was claiming to be God.

What can we learn from the way religious people responded to Jesus?

When people ask me, 'Show me where Jesus literally said he is God', I always tell them to look at the reaction of the monotheistic Jewish people when they heard Jesus' claims. Their reaction speaks volumes. It was provoked by their clear understanding of what Jesus said.

One day someone asked me where I came from. 'Have a guess,' I said. 'You are from Pakistan,' he answered. 'No. Let me give you some clues… My mother language is Arabic. My home county was a French colony. It is ruled by monarchy. It is in North West of Africa and only a few miles of the Mediterranean Sea separate it from Spain. Our national foods are Couscous and Tajin. The capital city is Rabat…' 'You are Moroccan,' my friend concluded. He was right. Though I hadn't said literally, 'I am Moroccan', my description was so clear that my friend immediately realized where I came from.

So it was with the religious people who heard Jesus' claims. He made clear claims that he was God. He claimed for himself divine titles which are exclusively reserved for God: 'I AM', 'The Son of Man' and 'The Son of God'. He also said he was one with God the Father. In each case, the Jews clearly understood Jesus' words and became furious, many times seeking to kill him, 'for blasphemy, and because you [Jesus], being a Man, make Yourself God'.

Can anyone really say in the light of this that Jesus never claimed to be God?!

4.

What does the character
of Jesus show us?

Jesus claimed divine names and titles for himself, but do his characteristics match up to those claims? There are certain things that are true about God that could never be true of you and me. Yet they are true of Jesus Christ. Here are six examples.

His holiness

Holiness means separation. Separation from evil. Uncontaminated by it. The Bible declares that Jesus was without sin. He 'committed no sin, nor was deceit found in His mouth' (Bible, 1 Peter 2:22). Jesus was 'holy, harmless, undefiled, separate from sinners' (Bible, Hebrews 7:26). The apostle Paul refers to Jesus as he 'who knew no sin' (Bible, 2 Corinthians 5:21). Jesus challenged his enemies, asking, 'Which of you convicts Me of sin?' (John 8:46). Even demons called Jesus 'the Holy One of God' (Bible, Luke 4:34).

Only God is holy!

His eternal existence

We have seen that Jesus, the Word, was there 'in the beginning' (John 1:1). In prayer to God the Father, Jesus spoke of 'the glory which I had with You before the world was' (Bible, John 17:5). Jesus is 'before all things, and in Him all things consist' (Bible, Colossians 1:17). As we have seen, the prophets spoke of Jesus as the 'Everlasting Father' (Bible, Isaiah 9:6), who existed 'from everlasting' (Bible, Micah 5:2).

Only God is eternal!

His unchanging nature

Look at the following statements about Jesus:

'Jesus Christ is the same yesterday, today, and for ever'
(Bible, Hebrews 13:8).

'They [the heavens and the earth] will perish, but You remain;
And they will all grow old like a garment;
Like a cloak You will fold them up,
And they will be changed.
But You are the same,
And Your years will not fail'
(Bible, Hebrews 1:11-12).

Only God is unchanging!

His infinite power

Jesus said, 'All authority has been given to Me in heaven and on earth' (Bible, Matthew 28:18). 'All things have been delivered to Me by My Father' (Bible, Matthew 11:27). He sustains 'all things by the word of His power' (Bible, Hebrews 1:3). He had the power to raise the dead to life (Bible, John 11:43-44; Luke 7:14). The final resurrection of all people will be accomplished through his power: 'Do not marvel at this; for the hour is coming in which all who are in the graves will hear His voice and come forth' (Bible, John 5:28).

> The final resurrection of all people will be accomplished through [Jesus'] power.

Only God is all powerful!

His infinite knowledge

Amazed by Jesus' teachings, his disciples said, 'You know all things' (Bible, John 16:30). On another occasion, Jesus asked the people, 'Why do you think evil in your hearts?' (Bible, Matthew 9:4). He could read their thoughts. Elsewhere we read, 'Jesus knew from the beginning who they were who did not believe, and who would betray Him' (Bible, John 6:64). In Christ 'are hidden all the treasures of wisdom and knowledge' (Colossians 2:3).

Jesus said, 'No one knows the Son except the Father. Nor does anyone know the Father except the Son…' (Bible, Matthew 11:27). Jesus alone knows God to perfection. His knowledge must therefore be infinite.

Only God knows everything!

His presence everywhere

Jesus himself declared that he is present everywhere. 'For where two or three are gathered together in My name, I am there in the midst of them' (Bible, Matthew 18:20). When Jesus met with his disciples on the Mount of Olives after his resurrection, he assured them of his continued presence and power. His influence with them would not be that of a dead teacher, but that of a living presence. 'I am with you always, even to the end of the age' (Matthew 28:20).

Since Jesus is always present, he is able to guard and comfort those who trust him. No suffering can come upon them except that which he sees to be for their ultimate good.

Only God is present everywhere!

5.

What do the actions of Jesus demonstrate?

Actions speak louder than words. It is all very well that the Bible gives Jesus divine names, titles and characteristics, but is it hypocrisy? Does Jesus also do things that only God can do?

His act of creation

We saw that John's Gospel and the apostle Paul call Jesus the Creator. Elsewhere we read, Jesus 'laid the foundation of the earth...' and the heavens are called the work of his hands (Bible, Hebrews 1:10). These words speak of God in the Psalms of David but in the book of Hebrews they are applied to Jesus. During his time on earth, Jesus gave further evidence that he is the one who formed the universe, by calming a raging storm with a word, and walking on water (Bible, Mark 4:39 and Mark 6:48).

God alone is the Creator of all things!

His being the source of life

Jesus is the one who gives life. John writes, 'In Him [Jesus] was *life*, and the life was the light of men' (Bible, John 1:4). Jesus himself stated, 'I am the way, the truth, and *the life*. No one comes to the Father except through Me' (Bible, John 14:6). 'I am the resurrection and *the life*. He who believes in Me, though he may die, he shall live' (Bible, John 11:25). 'For as the Father has *life* in Himself, so He has granted the Son to have *life* in Himself' (Bible, John 5:26). To demonstrate this, Jesus raised a number of people from the dead, such as Lazarus (Bible, John 11).

God alone is the source of life!

His reception of prayer and worship

To worship anyone but God is idolatry. The apostle Peter was once offered worship, but refused it in light of the Law that says, 'You shall worship the Lord your God, and Him only you shall serve' (cf. Bible, Acts 10:25-26).

An angel also refused to be worshipped (Bible, Revelation 22:8-9), yet we read that on numerous occasions Jesus received worship while he was on earth. The wise men, having been guided to the baby Jesus, 'fell down and worshipped Him' (Bible, Matthew 2:11). When Jesus went to the disciples walking on the water, those who were in the boat 'worshipped Him, saying, "Truly You are the Son of God,"' (Bible, Matthew 14:33).

Jesus restored the sight of a blind man, who later returned and 'worshipped Him' (Bible, John 9:38). When he saw Jesus after his resurrection, Thomas called him, 'My Lord and my God!' (Bible, John 20:28). Jesus did not rebuke Thomas.

After the resurrection, the disciples returned to Galilee. 'When they saw Him [Jesus], they worshipped Him' (Bible, Matthew 28:17). Jesus accepted such worship as perfectly right. He never rejected it as improper or misdirected.

Jesus told his disciples, 'Whatever you ask in My name, that I will do, that the Father may be glorified in the Son. If you ask anything in My name, I will do it' (Bible, John 14:13-14). By promising to hear and answer prayer, and by accepting worship, Jesus directly claimed to be God.

God alone is offered worship and prayer!

His authority to forgive sins

At one time, a paralysed man was brought to Jesus. The first thing Jesus said to him was 'Son, your sins are forgiven you.' Imagine the outrage felt by the religious leaders! They already questioned Jesus' authority and certainly did not believe that he had the right to forgive sins. Jesus knew what they were thinking, so he challenged them, 'Which is easier, to say to the paralytic, "*Your* sins are forgiven you," or to say, "Arise, take up your bed and walk"? But that you may know that the Son of Man has power on earth to forgive sins…' He told the paralysed man to stand up. The man got up, picked up his mat and walked home! (Bible, Mark 2:5-12).

Let me ask you a question. Imagine I punched you. Your friend then said to me: 'I forgive you.' Would that be normal? Of course not! Only you would have the right to forgive me. When Jesus forgave sin he was declaring himself to be God, since only God has the right to forgive sin. It is against God that all of us, without exception, have sinned. Therefore only God can pardon us and declare us forgiven. No person, priest or prophet can forgive sins. Moses said, 'The LORD is longsuffering and abundant in mercy, forgiving iniquity and transgression' (Bible, Numbers 14:18). David wrote, 'Bless the LORD, O my soul, and forget not all His benefits: who forgives all your iniquities' (Bible, Psalm 103:2-3). The prophet Daniel said, 'To the Lord our God belong mercy and forgiveness, though we have rebelled against Him' (Bible, Daniel 9:9).

When the prophet John the Baptist saw Jesus, he declared, 'Behold! The Lamb of God who takes away the sin of the world!' (Bible, John 1:29). Later, after the death of Jesus, the apostle Peter said, 'To Him [Jesus] all the prophets witness that, through His name, whoever believes in Him will receive remission [forgiveness] of sins' (Bible, Acts 10:43). John the Baptist, Peter and others could say that because they knew Jesus had the authority to forgive sin. He is God.

God alone can forgive sins!

His being the Saviour

The Bible says that only Jehovah, God, is our Saviour. For example, God said through Isaiah, 'I, even I, am the LORD [Jehovah], and besides Me there is no saviour' (Isaiah 43:11). God also spoke through another prophet called Hosea, saying, 'Yet I am the LORD your God ... there is no saviour besides Me' (Bible, Hosea 13:4).

Yet Jesus Christ is identified as our Saviour! Before the birth of Christ, an angel spoke to Joseph, the man who was engaged to be married to Mary, the mother of Jesus. 'Joseph, son of David, do not be afraid to take to you Mary your wife, for that which is conceived in her is of the Holy Spirit. And she will bring forth a Son, and you shall call His name JESUS, for *He will save* His people from their sins' (Bible, Matthew 1:20-21).

Later, when the baby Jesus was born in Bethlehem, angels appeared to some shepherds saying, 'Do not be afraid, for behold, I bring you good tidings of great joy which will be to all people. For there is born to you this day in the city of David *a Saviour, who is Christ the Lord*' (Bible, Luke 2:8-11). Many other passages such as Philippians 3:20; Titus 2:13; 3:6; 2 Peter 1:1; 2:20; 3:18, etc., identify Jesus as the Saviour.

> [Jesus] gave up his own sinless life ... taking the punishment we deserve.

Just before his crucifixion, Jesus made it plain that the pardon of sins would be accomplished through his death (Bible,

Matthew 26:28). He gave up his own sinless life in order to act as a substitute, taking the punishment we deserve.

God alone is the Saviour!

His being the Judge of the world

Jesus claims that he will one day return and judge the world. He said, 'For as the lightning comes from the east and flashes to the west, so also will the coming of the Son of Man be ... all the tribes of the earth will mourn, and they will see the Son of Man coming on the clouds of heaven with power and great glory' (Bible, Matthew 24:27, 30).

Jesus described how, at the end of time, he will judge all people. 'When the Son of Man comes in His glory, and all the holy angels with Him, then He will sit on the throne of His glory. All the nations will be gathered before Him, and He will separate them one from another, as a shepherd divides his sheep from the goats.' One category of people, the 'sheep', will be taken to the kingdom of God. To the others, Jesus will say, 'Depart from Me, you cursed, into the everlasting fire prepared for the devil and his angels' (Bible, Matthew 25:31-33, 41). The criterion by which people will be judged is the way they have responded to Jesus.

God alone is the Judge!

In his actions, therefore, Jesus did things that only God can do. He is able to satisfy the spiritual needs of all who trust in him.

6.

What did writers in the first centuries say about Jesus?

One commonly held myth is that Christianity as we know it today was not invented until the Council of Nicaea in A.D. 325. It is said that the early Christian church thought of Jesus Christ as a good moral teacher, but did not worship him until the fourth century when the Trinity and the deity of Christ were 'invented'. *The Da Vinci Code*, a book that has recently been made into a movie, makes this very claim (among other bizarre assertions). The author, Dan Brown, claims that no one in the early church believed that Jesus was God, but that this idea was invented and circulated by the Emperor Constantine who gained control of the Roman Empire in A.D. 312.

This claim is absolute nonsense. History is quite clear on the matter, and weighs heavily against Brown's view. Our examination of this question, using both biblical and secular sources, as well as the writings of the early church fathers, will clearly establish that Jesus was worshipped as God during the first century and early second century. The

Bible was completed in the first century and, as we have
seen, it clearly teaches the divinity of Jesus Christ. Let's
look at non-biblical proofs for the deity of Jesus Christ.

Early Christian sources

Many people acknowledge that the Bible says that Jesus is
God, but some allege that the Bible was edited long after
it was originally penned. Such claims fly in the face of
volumes of documents written by the early church fathers,
who liberally cited verses from the New Testament in their
own writings. Since many of these writings date from the
first and second centuries, claims that the Bible has been
rewritten are obviously false.

The following texts from Christian writers who lived
between New Testament times and the reign of Constantine
make it abundantly clear that belief in Christ's divinity and
equality with God the Father was an indisputable part of
the Christian tradition from the beginning — long before
the Council of Nicaea. These quotations are by no means
exhaustive — they are just a very limited selection.

Clement of Rome (A.D. 95). Clement of Rome wrote a
letter often referred to as the *Second Letter of Clement.* It
was probably written within a year or so of the apostle
John's death and begins, 'Brothers, we ought so to think of
Jesus Christ, *as of God.*'[1]

Ignatius (A.D. 30-107) was born before Christ's death and resurrection. He was the Bishop of Antioch and a disciple of the apostle John. Over time, he wrote seven letters. Six were addressed to various churches and the seventh to Polycarp, Bishop of Smyrna.[2] What follows are short excerpts from two of them.[3]

To the Ephesians: Ignatius opens his first letter by telling the Ephesian church it is '...united and elect in a true passion, by the will of the Father and of *Jesus Christ our GOD*'. He also called Jesus, '*GOD IN MAN*' (7:2). He continues: 'For *our God, Jesus Christ*, was, according to the appointment of God, conceived in the womb by Mary, of the seed of David, but by the Holy Ghost' (18:2,3).

Near the end of the letter, Ignatius describes the effect of Jesus' life on earth. 'From that time forward every sorcery and every spell was dissolved, the ignorance of wickedness vanished away ... when *GOD appeared in the likeness of man* unto the newness of everlasting life' (19:3).

To the Romans: Ignatius opens this letter, '...to the church that is beloved and enlightened through the will of Him who willed all things that are, by faith and love toward *Jesus Christ our GOD* ... abundant greetings in *Jesus Christ our GOD* in blamelessness' (introduction).

The fact that Ignatius was not rebuked, nor branded as teaching heresy by any of the churches, proves that the early church, long before A.D. 107, accepted the deity of Christ.

Polycarp (A.D. 69-155) was another disciple of the apostle
John. After Ignatius was executed, Polycarp collected
together Ignatius' seven letters and sent them to the
church at Philippi at their request. He also added one of
his own.[4]

   In his letter, Polycarp tells the Philippians they can 'gain
great advantage' by reading the letters of Ignatius (13:2).
He clearly supported Ignatius' teaching, and he prayed,
'...may He (God the Father) grant unto you a lot with and
portion among His saints, and to us with you, and to all
that are under heaven, who shall believe on *our Lord and
GOD Jesus Christ* and on His Father that raised Him from
the dead' (12:2).

Justin Martyr (ca A.D. 100-165). As his name implies,
Justin was executed for his faith. His major work is now
known as *The First Apology of Justin Martyr.* In this book,
he refers to Jesus as the Word (Greek '*Logos*', see John 1:1).
He states that the church proclaims, '...the teachings of
the Logos, because *He is divine...* It is only reasonable that
we worship Him...'[5]

   Justin further declares, '...the Father of the universe
has a Son, who — since He is the First-Begotten *Logos*
[Word] of God — *is true Deity*'.[6] Elsewhere, in his book,
Dialogue with Trypho, Justin proclaims, 'For Christ is
King, and Priest, and GOD and Lord...'[7]

Tatian (ca A.D. 110-172), who defended the truth of the
Christian faith, wrote, 'We do not act as fools, O Greeks,

nor utter idle tales when we announce that *God was born in the form of man.*[8]

Melito (died A.D. 190), Bishop of Sardis, was active during the reign of Marcus Aurelius. In his 'Homily on the Passion', Melito exclaims: '…He rose from the dead as GOD, being by nature GOD AND MAN… This is Jesus Christ, to whom belongs the glory to the ages. Amen.'[9]

Irenaeus (A.D. 120-202) wrote that Jesus was 'perfect God and perfect man'; 'not a mere man … but was very God'; and that 'He is in Himself in His own right … God, and Lord, and King Eternal'.[10]

Tertullian (A.D. 145-220). In Tertullian's day, Christians were being charged with being '…worshippers of a mere human being'. Tertullian responded: 'We must make, therefore, a remark or two about Christ's divinity.' He continues: 'He is *the Son of God and is called GOD* from unity of substance with God. For God, too, is a Spirit… Thus Christ is Spirit of Spirit and GOD OF GOD … in His birth GOD AND MAN united.' Later in the book, he asserts: 'Surely Christ has a right to reveal Deity, which was in fact His own essential possession.'[11]

Clement of Alexandria (ca A.D. 210) wrote: 'This Word, then, the Christ, the cause of both our being at first (for He was in God) and of our well-being, this very Word has now appeared as man, *He alone being both, God and man* — that Author of all blessings to us... This is the New Song, the manifestation of the Word that was in the beginning, and before the beginning.'[12]

These are only a few of the references that we could include as evidence in support of Christ's deity.

Secular sources — testimonies from hostile sources

In the case for Christ's deity, the value of evidence, particularly from hostile sources, is tremendous. Hostile sources are the testimonies of those who were definitely not followers of Christ; i.e., people who had no interest in propagating favourable belief in him. Yet, they themselves affirm that early Christians believed in the divinity of Jesus Christ.

Pliny the Younger

Pliny the Younger, governor of Pontus/Bithynia from A.D. 111-113, wrote to Emperor Trajan[13] regarding the early Christian church. After asking people three times whether they were Christians, those who persisted were executed, 'For I had no doubt that, whatever the nature of their creed, stubbornness and inflexible obstinacy surely deserve to be punished.' Some of the people Pliny interrogated 'denied that they were or had been Christians ... offered prayer with incense' to the image of Emperor Trajan and cursed Christ. Pliny continues: 'They asserted, however, that the sum and substance of their fault or error had been that they were accustomed to meet on a fixed day before dawn and *sing responsively a hymn to Christ as to a god*,[14] and to bind themselves by oath, not to some crime, but not to commit fraud, theft, or adultery, nor falsify their trust, nor to refuse to return a trust when called upon to do so.'[15]

Pliny was dealing with a situation that was in full swing. Many Christians refused to worship the Roman emperor as a god, but instead worshipped a man called 'Christ'.

So what does this prove (if anything) about Christianity?

We have here strong, non-biblical evidence that there were first and second-century people who believed that Jesus was God and were willing to die for that belief. Pliny confirms that there were Christians who believed Christ to be 'as a god' as early as A.D. 112. Clearly even the Romans knew that Jesus was being worshipped and wanted to 'check and cure' 'the contagion of this superstition' that had 'spread not only to the cities but also to the villages and farms'.

So what, you ask?

Well, this proves that belief in Jesus' divinity goes back way before the Council of Nicaea in the fourth century

> Many Christians refused to worship the Roman emperor as a god, but instead worshipped a man called 'Christ'.

AD. In fact, it places belief in Jesus' divinity in the *first century*! Pliny quoted what his captives said about what they used to do before they stopped being Christians, i.e. between three and twenty years earlier. Twenty years earlier would take us back to around A.D. 92, well into the first century. Furthermore, if Pliny executed people for embracing Jesus' divinity in A.D. 112, the religion or movement must have begun before that. Roman historian Suetonius confirms the presence of Christians in Rome as early as the late 40s and their willingness to die for their beliefs as early as A.D. 64.

Lucian of Samosata

Another source comes from Lucian of Samosata who was a second-century Greek satirist. In one of his writings, dating from A.D. 170, he notes as follows: 'The Christians ... worship a man to this day — the distinguished personage who introduced their novel rites, and was crucified on that account... You see, these misguided creatures start with the general conviction that they are immortal ... and then it was impressed on them by their original lawgiver that they are all brothers, from the moment that they are converted, and deny the gods of Greece, and worship the crucified sage, and live after his laws. All this they take quite on faith...'[16]

We know the man Lucian is writing about, and that man is Jesus. What did Jesus teach? He taught that men are brothers from the moment of conversion, which meant denying Greek gods, worshipping Jesus, and living according to his teachings. Though Lucian opposed Christianity, he acknowledges the historicity of Jesus, that he was crucified, that Christians worship him, and that this is done by faith.

Archaeology

Alexamenos graffiti

Another secular source indicating that Christians were recognized as those who worshipped Jesus before the fourth century is seen in some first-century (or early second-century) Pagan graffiti. In 1857, archaeologists discovered graffiti scratched into the plaster walls of a Roman barracks probably built by the Emperor Nero. The caricature was designed only a few years after the apostles first preached

the gospel in Rome. It ridicules Christians by depicting a believer with arms raised in adoration and worship of a horse-headed god crucified on a cross. Below it, there is an inscription scratched very crudely into the wall. The inscription reads: ALEXAMENOS SEBETE THEON, *'Alexamenos*

Graffiti found in Rome   *worships god'.*

The graffiti reflects the common attitude of the day to
the gospel and those who called themselves Christians.
The gospel's message of Christ crucified was a stumbling
block to the Jews, and foolishness to the Greek-speaking
world. But it does show that early Christians worshipped
Jesus as God.

Megiddo prison

Further archaeological evidence proving that Jesus was
worshipped before the fourth century was recently
discovered in Megiddo, Israel.

While prisoners were digging to expand the Israeli
prison at Megiddo, they found a large tiled floor. Further
excavation revealed the remnants of the walls of a church,
within a larger Roman villa. In addition to beautiful fish
mosaics (the original symbol of Christianity), a number
of inlaid inscriptions were found on the tiles. The site was
dated to the first half of the third century through pottery
remnants and the style of Greek writing in the inscriptions.
One inscription indicated that Gaianus, a Roman military
officer, helped pay for the mosaic. A second inscription
was in remembrance of four Christian women (maybe
martyrs?) — three with Greek names, and the fourth with
a Roman name. However, the most compelling inscription is the one that was a tribute to Jesus, 'Akeptous, the
God-loving, offered this table for [the] God Jesus Christ,
as a remembrance'.

Obviously, the discovery of a third-century inscription calling Jesus God discredits the idea that Jesus was not worshipped until the fourth century!

Conclusion

In conclusion, from the very first, church leaders — immediately after the time of the apostles up to the Council of Nicaea in the fourth century and beyond — have consistently believed and taught that Jesus Christ is God. Therefore, Dan Brown and others are clearly mistaken when they maintain that the divinity of Jesus was 'invented' by Christians in the fourth century.

Only one logical explanation can be given for this abundant early testimony to the deity of Jesus Christ. Early church leaders were simply declaring what had already been declared by Jesus Christ and the apostles in Holy Scripture — that Jesus Christ was indeed God.

7.

What impact has Jesus had on real lives?

The dramatic effect that Jesus has had on people's lives indicates that his claims are true. Nobody has changed the world the way Jesus has. Nobody! Charles Bradlaugh, the nineteenth-century atheist, once challenged Hugh Price Hughes, a well-known Christian minister, to debate with him about the claims of Christianity compared with those of atheism. Hughes agreed on one condition: that Bradlaugh bring with him a hundred people whose lives had been changed for the better by their commitment to atheism. Hughes said he would bring a hundred whose lives had been changed for the better by their commitment to Christianity. But Bradlaugh couldn't face the challenge! Hughes then dropped the demand to fifty, then to twenty, then to ten, and finally to just one. Even then Bradlaugh withdrew from the challenge. He could not produce one atheist who would qualify!

The following experiences of people from all walks of life demonstrate the unity of Christian experience. While each one has a different background, profession or culture, all point to the same object as the source of new power for transformed lives — Jesus Christ. Multiply these testimonies by millions upon millions and you would begin to approach something like the impact Christ has had on the world in the past two thousand years.

Is the Christian experience valid? These and millions more believe so, and have new lives to back up their statement.

Throughout history

The influence which Jesus has had on people's lives has never been surpassed. No other great leader has inspired so many positive changes in the lives of his followers. People who encounter the risen Christ are totally transformed. Their outlook on life is altered for ever. Staying true to their faith, they do not hesitate to face hardship, persecution and even death. Many consecrate their lives to serving others, minimizing their own needs and desires.

First-century Christians

Following Jesus' crucifixion, his disciples were devastated. They had forsaken him in the Garden of Gethsemane to save their own lives. But after they met the resurrected Christ, they were radically changed. Suddenly, they were willing to give their lives to tell Jesus' story to the world. Many were tortured and killed because they proclaimed that Jesus was alive.

Peter

When Jesus told his disciples that he would be arrested, put to death and they would all desert him, Peter replied, 'I never will.' He was certain that he, of all people, would not be so frightened that he would forsake his Lord. However, Jesus knew Peter's heart better than this disciple knew it himself. The prophet Jeremiah said, 'The heart is deceitful above all things, and desperately wicked' (Bible, Jeremiah 17:9). Peter was so convinced, 'I will lay down my life for Your sake' (Bible, John 13:37). Yet, when Jesus was arrested, Peter denied him three times! In his third, and most vehement, denial he swore that he had no connection with Jesus. What do you think Jesus' reaction was? We could understand it if Jesus had no desire to have anything to do with him after such a denial. Jesus 'turned and looked at Peter' (Bible, Luke 22:61). I am sure that it was a look of love, even though Peter had done such an awful thing. We are told that Peter shed tears of remorse and repentance. There is no doubt that he was genuinely sorry for his behaviour.

Certainly Jesus Christ had not cast him aside, even though Peter must have felt that he deserved to be cast off and forbidden to serve his Lord. We know Jesus did not adopt such an attitude because when he rose from the dead the angel gave this message to the women who came to Jesus' tomb: 'Do not be alarmed. You seek Jesus of Nazareth, who was crucified. He is risen! He is not here. See the place where they laid Him. But go, tell His disciples — and Peter — that He is going before you into Galilee; there you will see Him, as He said to you' (Bible, Mark 16:6-7). It is as though Jesus was saying, 'Make sure that Peter gets the message. I want him back in my service.' Peter was restored. He was changed by the power of Jesus Christ. Later we hear of Peter receiving the Holy Spirit and speaking boldly about Jesus in front of orthodox Jews (before whom he had denied any connection with Jesus). He was put into prison and was now willing to give his life for the sake of Jesus Christ. What would change a person so radically in this way? The power of Jesus!

James

Sceptics and enemies were also transformed. Jesus' younger half-brother, James, did not think Jesus was anybody special. He would not believe a word of what Jesus said. He thought Jesus was mad! But after the resurrected Jesus appeared to him, James not only believed Jesus was Lord but became the leader of the Jerusalem church and died as a martyr in A.D. 62.

Paul

Saul of Tarsus was the chief persecutor of early Christians. A very zealous Jew, he was an enemy to the Christian church. He was a murderer. He put innocent Christian people in prison and delighted in doing so. He hated Jesus Christ and his name and his people and his work and his word. But he had a dramatic encounter with the risen Christ. As Saul was on his way to Damascus, filled with threats and fury, he was stopped in his tracks by Jesus Christ himself who said, 'Saul, Saul, why are you persecuting Me?' (Bible, Acts 9:4). It was Jesus' call which changed him. He was transformed from Saul, the enemy of Christianity, to Paul, the main propagator of its message. He left his position of prestige in Jewish society, to become a travelling missionary who experienced incredible suffering in order to share the message of Christ throughout the Roman Empire.

Roman governor Plinius Secundus wrote in his *Epistles X96* that Christians were people who loved the truth at any cost. Although he was ordered to torture and execute them for refusing to curse Jesus, he was continually amazed and impressed with their firm commitments 'not to do any wicked deeds, never to commit any fraud, theft, adultery, never to falsify their word, not to deny a trust when they should be called upon to deliver it up'.

For centuries, true Christians around the world have stood as shining examples of the standards of truth and love established by Jesus of Nazareth.

Modern-day Christianity

The power of Christ knows no boundary of time or space. In our own age, many sceptics have been convinced just as thoroughly as their first-century counterparts.

Lew Wallace — a sceptic who was saved

For example, Lew Wallace, a famous general and literary genius, was a known atheist. For two years, Wallace studied in the leading libraries of Europe and America, seeking information that would destroy Christianity for ever. While writing the second chapter of a book outlining his arguments, he suddenly found himself on his knees crying out to Jesus, 'My Lord and my God!' (Bible, John 20:28).

When confronted by solid indisputable evidence, he could no longer deny that Jesus Christ was the Son of God. Later, Lew Wallace wrote the book *Ben Hur*, one of the greatest English novels ever written concerning the time of Christ.

Leo D'Arcangelo — former criminal

Pacing back and forth in his prison cell, Leo D'Arcangelo was deeply disturbed. Who wouldn't be, facing what was ahead of him? As a boy of eleven, he had snatched a lady's handbag on a crowded tram. That was the start. Five years of stealing followed before his first arrest at sixteen in a Philadelphia department store. Shortly after release he started trafficking heroin. Then began the seemingly endless arrests: November 1954, for use and possession of drugs; January 1955, for picking pockets. Shortly after, in Los Angeles, Leo was arrested for jumping bail.

As he paced his cell he noticed a few lines crudely scrawled on the wall:

When you come to the end of your journey and this trouble is racked in your mind, and there seems no other way out than by just mourning, turn to Jesus, for it is him that you must find.

This started him thinking: 'This is the end of my journey. What have I got to show for it? Nothing except a lousy past and a worse future. Jesus, I need your help. I've made a mess of my life and this is the end of the journey, and all the crying isn't going to change my past. Jesus, if you can change my life, please do it. Help me make tomorrow different.'

For the first time Leo felt something besides despair.

Released from prison in September 1958 a totally changed man, Leo earned his high school diploma and then went on to graduate from West Chester State College and the Reformed Episcopal Seminary in Philadelphia.

He is presently active in prison work and as a speaker in church and youth meetings.

Kamal — a radical Egyptian terrorist changed from a murderous person to a forgiving person

Kamal started memorizing the Qur'an at a very early age and developed what he called 'a love for the word of God'.

As he grew older, he started reading books on Islam and the interpretation of the Qur'an. By sorting out Muslims from non-Muslims according to the Qur'an's teaching, he ended up considering his own parents 'infidels'. Little things such as a woman not wearing a veil would make her a non-Muslim according to the way he understood the Qur'an. If a man didn't grow a beard he would be treated as a non-Muslim. He considered Christians as his worst enemies and started getting involved in attacks against Christians and churches. An Islamic group, dedicated to the overthrow of the secular government of Egypt and the installation of a strict Muslim government, recruited him into their ranks, appointing him as a local leader. His group became involved in kidnapping a famous moderate Muslim writer who had dared to criticize the Islamic group.

Upon reading an article in the Cairo newspaper about Christians arrested in Egypt for proselytizing, Kamal and his group decided that it was 'past time' to do something for the sake of Islam. Given their small numbers, however, they decided their battle would be an intellectual one, researching and writing a book proving that Mohammed is the true prophet of God, and that the Bible of the Christians and Jews is a corrupted text. Kamal was chosen by his Emir (leader), the leader of the Islamic group, to do the research and write the book. He objected strenuously at first, but eventually took on the job, which he described as the 'most distasteful thing' he had ever done.

When he had completed reading the Bible and cross-referencing what he had read with numerous Islamic books, Kamal was astonished to discover that the Bible was neither inaccurate nor corrupted. Instead, he was amazed at the Bible's teachings on forgiveness and unconditional love, as reflected in the life and words of Jesus. He was particularly stunned to read how Jesus had warned his followers about persecution and how, two thousand years later, that persecution was taking place exactly as Jesus had said it would. His reading of the Bible helped him to understand why Christians in Egypt never retaliated against Muslims, and why they were able to forgive and forget. As much as he hated reading the Bible, he fell in love with its message and teachings.

Nonetheless, he had a job to do, and he continued with dogged determination, electing to prove that Jesus is not God and was never crucified. Studying the Qur'an for this purpose, he put together all of God's qualities and attributes as the Qur'an talks about them, and then searched the Qur'an for Jesus' attributes. To his shock, Kamal discovered that many attributes the Qur'an assigns to God are also assigned to Jesus, proving to Kamal that Jesus and God are, indeed, one.

Growing doubts now made Kamal's life miserable. He had always loved Islam and believed that the only way to God was through Mohammed. But if Jesus and God are one, then what is the way to heaven?

One day, the Emir came to visit Kamal in his house and discovered all the research that Kamal had documented (the deity of Jesus, the Bible being the true Word of God, etc.). He couldn't believe what he read. He told Kamal that he would kill him if he shared his heretical ideas with any Muslim and that he was now considered an infidel.

Kamal, however, could not turn from the conviction that Christianity was the right way. He sat down and said, 'God, you know that I love you, and I know that you want me on the right path. God, I can't resist anymore. All that I did, I did trying to please you. Please help me.'

Jesus heard his prayer. He saved him. He gave him a new heart and new life. Kamal's search for reconciliation started with his mother. He begged her forgiveness for his years of harshness and ill treatment of the family. His search for reconciliation didn't end with his family either. He sought out the Christian owners of businesses whom he had robbed, or mistreated, and begged their forgiveness too.

Over the ensuing months, Kamal grew in his new faith, gradually winning the confidence and trust of local Christians and finding fellowship at a church. He was baptized and continues to brave physical attacks and threats against his life, because he feels that no price is too great to pay for the one who gave everything for him, Jesus.

Joon Gon Kim — a Korean who loved his enemies

Many other men and women in recent decades have dedicated their lives to spreading the Christian message, often braving torture and death. For example, in Korea, Joon Gon Kim, a well-known Christian leader, witnessed his wife and father being slaughtered before his eyes by Communist sympathizers from his own village. He himself was beaten senseless and left for dead. He survived the beating and asked God to give him love for the souls of his enemies. He was eventually instrumental in the conversion of thirty Communists to Christ, including the person responsible for the death of his family members.

Yes, Jesus always has, and still does, change lives. He alone has the power to do that life-transforming work in people's hearts. All of the above Christians have found fulfilment and joy in following the teachings of Jesus. They were transformed when they met Christ and yielded their lives to him. Each of them has made a positive impact on the world. They realize that religion, agnosticism, atheism and secular humanism hold no true answers. Christianity is still relevant to the needs of today.

A reformed alcoholic, with vivid memories of past hopelessness and a new sense of power through Christ, was replying to the charge that 'his religion was a delusion'. He said, 'Thank God for the delusion; it has put clothes on my children, shoes on their feet and bread in their mouths. It has made a man of me and has put joy and peace in my home, which before had been a hell. If it is a delusion, may God send it to the slaves of drink everywhere, for their slavery is an awful reality.'

You may also wish to encounter the living God and experience his transforming power. Christ's desire is to enter your heart and give you a new life in him.

Conclusion:

So, who do you say Jesus is?

Each person has to confront Jesus' question, 'Who do you say that I am?' To answer this question is to come face-to-face with Jesus Christ. The good news is that in the face of Jesus Christ we see the very face of God, the one who has decided to be with us and for us, in spite of our sin.

The Bible and the earliest Christian documents are full of clear indications that Jesus is both Man and God — his divine names, unity with the Father, holiness, sinless life, ability to forgive sin and change lives, his acceptance of worship, his infinite power and knowledge... Remember the many miracles Jesus performed: he raised the dead; healed the lame, the blind, the deaf and the dumb, and the lepers; he cast out demons; and was the only person who ever lived without doing wrong. He walked on water, stilled the storm, multiplied a few pieces of bread and fish to feed multitudes, and rose from the dead. At last he ascended bodily to heaven before the eyes of his followers. These are all signs of his deity.

While visiting London the other day, I went to a bookshop to browse the Judaism section as I was interested in what Jewish writers say about Jesus. I picked up one book, read the contents page and went straight to the chapter that interested me. The author said something to the effect that the way Jesus is presented by the authors of the Christian's book puts him in a position equal to Jehovah (God). But the question is, asks the author: 'Was there really a historical Jesus? No one can prove to me that there was a historical Jesus of Nazareth. If there was a historical Jesus, I would not hesitate to trust him as my God!'

This is a very extraordinary claim by a Jew. It is so easy to prove the historicity of Jesus. Yet it is interesting to notice that this man *does* understand that the New Testament portrays Jesus in a way that leaves us in no doubt that he is God.

The late C. S. Lewis, famous professor at Oxford and Cambridge universities in England, and the author of the *Chronicles of Narnia*, was an agnostic who denied the deity of Christ for years. But he, in intellectual honesty, submitted to Jesus as his God and Saviour after studying the overwhelming evidence for his deity. He observed: 'You must make your choice. Either this man [Jesus] was, and is, the Son of God; or else a madman or something worse. You can shut Him up for a fool, you can spit at Him and kill Him as a demon; or you can fall at His feet and call Him Lord and God. But let us not come up with any patronizing nonsense about His being a great human teacher. He has not left that open to us. He did not intend to.'[1]

If the biblical claims of Jesus are true, he is God! Therefore, he is able to fulfil what he promised: 'Come to Me, all you who labour and are heavy laden, and I will give you rest. Take My yoke upon you and learn from Me … and you will find rest for your souls' (Bible, Matthew 11:28-29).

As we conclude, there are a few questions we should now ask.

Did God cease to be God when he came in the form of man?

Did Jesus cease to be what he was — God? No! He remains exactly what he was without any alteration. Has he become what he was not? Yes, he has. Is it subtraction? No, it is not. It is addition. God became a man. Has God been lessened? No. Has God somehow been spoiled? Not at all.

God once spoke to the prophet Moses from a bush. Did he stop being God then? Of course not. God cannot be limited by anything. When God revealed himself in the form of a man, he was not limited by his humanity. He continued to rule the universe. He continued to be what he always had been (God), but in Jesus, he also became what he had never previously been (man). Jesus Christ was not 50% God and 50% man. He was 100% God and

100% man — fully God and fully man. The divine person took upon himself a human nature. We really cannot understand the mystery of how this happened. But it is conceivable, certainly, that God has the power to add to himself a human nature and do it in such a way as to unite two natures in one person.

Imagine a brilliant light. Now imagine that the light is put inside a glass. Does the glass stop the light shining? No! In fact, as the light is reflected by the glass, it shines even more brightly. In a similar way, when God became man in the person of Jesus Christ, the body did not stop him being God. Jesus said, 'I am the light of the world.' God became what he had never previously been (man) but he continued to shine and to rule the universe. In this way, he revealed himself to the world *more clearly*.

Why did God come in the likeness of men?

Why did God have to become man? What was the point? This is a very important question. It is the heart of Christianity. To know the answer, we must go back to the beginning of creation. We need to grasp what happened in the Garden of Eden.

How did it all begin?

Everything about the world that God made was good. There was plenty of food and drink for every living creature. In this lovely setting the first people, Adam and Eve, lived. God told them that as long as they lived for him, obeying him, they would live for ever, but that if they disobeyed him they would surely die.

God wanted them to be his friends and to look after the earth and everything in it. God gave them a precious gift: free will. He did not make them like robots or machines so that they would have to love and obey him. Love must come freely. This gift of free will was one of the main differences between humankind and the animals. Adam and Eve could choose between right and wrong, good and bad. They could choose to love each other or not, to do what God wanted or what they wanted, to live for God or for themselves.

They chose to disobey God. They preferred to please themselves rather than God.

Why did they do this? What went wrong?

All evil and wrong come from the devil. Even the word 'devil' has the word 'evil' in it. While everyone today believes that evil exists, belief in a personal devil has declined. Isn't he just a comic figure with horns and a curly tail?

The Bible tells us to take the devil seriously. It tells us that, far from being a comic figure, he was once a glorious angel in heaven. His name then was Lucifer, which means 'one who bears light'. He became proud and jealous, wanting to be like God. He was banished from God's presence and now does all he can to turn men and women against God.

It was the devil, Satan (a name which means 'the deceiver'), who tempted the first man and woman to choose wrong and disobey God.

So in this way sin and wrong entered into our world and into human life.

At first Adam and Eve had walked with God in a loving relationship. But when they disobeyed, sin formed a vast, insurmountable chasm between them and God. We call this 'spiritual death'. It is because Adam became spiritually dead that he died physically several hundred years later.

As a result of what happened in the Garden of Eden, all of us are born with an infinite gap between us and God. The prophet David wrote, 'Behold, I was brought forth in iniquity, and in sin my mother conceived me' (Bible, Psalm 51:5). God is holy and we are sinful, so we are cut off from him. 'Your iniquities have separated you from your God; and your sins have hidden His face from you,' (Bible, Isaiah 59:2).

Because people listen to the devil's lies, they go his evil, selfish way. It is this that causes all the crime and wrong and suffering in the world. This is why there is so much evil, so many broken relationships, so much selfishness and greed. We are all by nature self-centred rather than God-centred. There is no exception to this, 'for all have sinned and fall short of the glory of God' (Bible, Romans 3:23).

> By nature we are separated from God.
> It is our disobedience which separates us.

It is a disease we all have and it affects not just us, but everyone we come into contact with. The Bible calls this 'sin'. This is what is wrong with the world, and that includes you and me.

By nature we are separated from God. It is our disobedience which separates us. Every man is sinful at heart; though someone may seem to be very holy outwardly, there remain sins of wrong motives, sins of the mind.

What is the solution?

Is there any hope? Many people try to bridge the gap by their own efforts. Some think they can get to God by being good religious people. They hope that their good deeds will outweigh their bad deeds enough to get them into paradise. But they never succeed. No one is perfect. It is not even that their contribution 'nearly but not quite' reaches God. The reality is that we fall infinitely short of the requirements. We can never reach God's standard by our own efforts. No matter how righteous we try to be, we are condemned: 'For whoever shall keep the whole law, and yet stumbles in one point, he is guilty of all' (Bible, James 2:10). Our sins can never be forgiven by striving toward self-righteousness. The huge chasm between us and God is still there.

The question remains: what is the solution?

Once, when I was sitting quietly, I saw a troop of ants marching up and down a wall. They were trying to carry a grain of wheat to the top; but without success. The grain of wheat was too heavy. The pull of gravity was greater than their efforts! I pitied them. I wondered how I could help those hopeless ants. If I had reached down with my hand, I might have squashed some of them by mistake. They would have run away in fear. I could not help them. The only way I could have helped them was by becoming an ant, while keeping my human strength! Only that way could I help without terrifying them.

We are a bit like those ants. We can never reach God by our own efforts and good works. The gravity of our sin is too great. It is stronger than our efforts. Sin weighs heavily on our shoulders. But God pitied and loved us. To liberate us from the tyranny of sin, he came in our likeness. He came as a man, but lived without sin. That was the main difference between him and us. Who can re-establish the broken relationship between God and man? Surely, the only one who can bridge the gap is one who is both God and man.

My sins are not serious!

Let me tell you about what happened to a friend of mine. His name is Olivier. When he told me that he once went to prison for failing to pay parking tickets, I asked: 'Why didn't you just pay them?'

He answered, 'They were just "parking tickets"; it was no big deal.'

Then he told me that the police arrived at his home at 4.00am, put him in a van and took him to court. As he stood before the judge, he said, 'Your honour, I have brought 500 francs with me to pay for the tickets and to cover the court costs.'

The judge said, 'Monsieur Argaud, I'm going to save you all that money. *You are going to jail*!'

Olivier was terrified. His big mistake was that he trivialized his crimes by thinking that they were 'just' parking tickets, and so he deceived himself. Had he known the judge's ruling (that he would go to prison), he would have immediately made things right between himself and the law.

Most of us realize that we have broken God's Law, the Ten Commandments, but we think it's no big deal. So, let me ask you a few questions about the Law you have broken and see if it *is* a big deal.

Have you ever lied? You say, 'Yes. But they were only white lies. They were nothing serious.'

Have you ever stolen something? You say, 'Yes, but only little things.'

Can you see what you are doing? You are *trivializing* your crimes, and like Olivier, you *will* deceive yourself. What you are doing is saying that you haven't actually 'sinned'. But the Bible warns, 'He who says he has no sin *deceives* himself.' The truth is that if you have lied, then you are a liar. If you have stolen anything (the value of the item stolen is irrelevant), you are a thief.

What you need to hear is the judge's ruling for lying and stealing. Here it is: 'All liars shall have their part in the lake which burns of fire' (Bible, Revelation 21:8). All liars go to hell and no thief will enter heaven. Not one (Bible, 1 Corinthians 6:9-10).

Now look at this: Jesus said, 'Whoever looks at a woman to lust for her has already committed adultery with her in his heart' (Bible, Matthew 5:28). Have you ever looked with lust? Then you have committed adultery as far as God is concerned. Have you used God's name as a swear word to express disgust? If you have, then you have used his holy name in vain. That is called 'blasphemy', and it is very serious in God's sight.

So if you have been honest enough to admit that you have broken those commandments, you are a self-admitted lying, thieving, blasphemous adulterer at heart. If God gives you justice on the Judgement Day, you will be guilty and end up in hell. Think of it — if you died right now, you would end up in hell... for ever. So, what are you going to do? How can you make things right between you and the Law?

Can religion help?

Absolutely not!

There are millions of people on this earth who have never seen the serious nature of sin. They are in the dark about the Judge's ruling. They have no idea that they will end up in hell for crimes that they consider trivial. They know that they have to face God after death, but they think that their religious works (like Olivier with his 500 francs) will buy their way out of any trouble in which they may find themselves. And as long as they trivialize their sin, they will deceive themselves into thinking that they can work their way into heaven by their religious works. It is as futile as a man who tried to row against the river. He was in a boat caught in fast-moving water, heading for a massive waterfall with jagged rocks 150 feet below. A passer-by saw him rowing against the current, but his efforts were futile. Minute by minute he was drawn closer and closer to the roaring falls. The passer-by ran to his car, grabbed a rope from the boot and threw it to the boat. When it fell across the bow, he shouted, 'Grab the rope. I will pull you to the shore!' He couldn't believe his eyes, for the man in the boat took no notice. He just kept on rowing frantically against the current, until he disappeared over the edge of the falls to his death.

God is our only hope!

God himself has thrown us a rope in Jesus Christ. He is the only one who can save us from death and hell. But we must let go of our own efforts to save ourselves and take hold of the rope. The moment we cease our own religious 'rowing' and have faith in Jesus, we find peace with God. The Bible says, 'For by grace you have been saved through faith, and that not of yourselves; it is the gift of God, not of works, lest anyone should boast' (Bible, Ephesians 2:8-9).

Let me give you another illustration to show that religion can never save you. Imagine that one day you go swimming and jump into deep water. You find yourself in trouble. Drowning! You are dying, but you cannot save yourself because you are completely out of your depth. You are hopeless and helpless. You shout for help. Someone approaches and yells, 'Pull yourself together and save yourself! Come on mate, do it yourself!' What a terrible thing to say to a drowning man! A second person arrives on the scene and actually jumps into the water. He starts swimming. He says, 'Look at me. Watch me and do the same. Then you will save yourself.' How ridiculous! There is no time for you to learn. In fact, a drowning man is absolutely incapable of learning anything. Now a third person approaches. He dives into the water, grabs you and drags you out of danger. You might resist him, but out of compassion he saves you from death. Now, which one of these three people would you thank the most? Surely the third one.

Religion is like the first two people. By nature we are drowning in our sin. We are in a mess because of our separation from God. Religion tells us, 'Save yourself. Do this and that. Don't do this or that and you will be saved.' Some religious leaders are seen as examples. Their followers are told that if they imitate their lifestyle, they will be saved. It is like the second person who jumps into the water.

So religion cannot save us. We are hopeless. The Bible says that we are incapable of saving ourselves. That is why we need someone to jump into the water of our life and get hold of us and save us from our sin. This is exactly what God has done. He has provided a way for sinners to be brought back to him. God says to us, 'I know your situation. I know that you are separated from me. I know that your life is in a mess. I know that you cannot save yourself. And I know that giving you laws and commandments will not save you because you cannot and do not do them. You are incapable of fulfilling them. But, I will come to where you are and get you out of the tyranny of your sin.' So God came to this world in the person of Jesus Christ. 'For Christ also suffered once for sins, the just for the unjust, that He might bring us to God,' (Bible, 1 Peter 3:18). When Jesus died on the cross, he died as our perfect human substitute. He took the punishment that we deserve for our sin. He bridged the insurmountable chasm that separates us from God. But how could one man be the substitute for so many people? Since Jesus is also the divine Son of God, his sacrifice was enough to cover the sins of all those who believe in him. To sin against the infinite God is to sin infinitely and therefore to deserve infinite punishment. Left to ourselves we are lost. Only Jesus, the infinite Son of God, was able to take that infinite punishment in our place.

It is unwise to reject God's saving plan. What do you think of the rower who refused to be saved?

When someone submits themselves to Jesus (by trusting in his death and resurrection), Jesus forgives their sin and grants them a place in paradise. He will dismiss the case against them.

Why was Jesus' death necessary?

Let us get it clear that Jesus was dead — beyond any shadow of a doubt. He was certified as dead by the centurion in charge of the execution squad. He was recognized as dead by Pilate, the governor (who gave permission for a friend to bury his body). And the crowning proof is that when a spear was thrust into his side under his heart in order to make sure he was dead, out came what an eyewitness called blood and water (Bible, John 19:34-37). Obviously the scientific explanation of this was unknown to men of those days, but the diagnosis is clear. Dark blood and light serum came from the body of Jesus, and the separation of clot from serum in the blood is the strongest medical proof that the patient is dead. So don't be taken in by any of the 'swoon' theories which allege that Jesus was not quite dead but recovered in the cool of the tomb! He most certainly *was* dead.

But why did Christ need to die? Could he not have saved us without dying? Man had broken God's Law and the penalty was death: physical and spiritual. 'The wages of sin is death' (Bible, Romans 6:23). How could Jesus Christ deliver us without meeting our full penalty?

Death is man's big problem. If anyone was to save us, he would have to resolve this problem. He would have to conquer death. He would have to restore our broken relationship with God.

When Adam and Eve disobeyed, God immediately promised to send them a Saviour. Through that Saviour's suffering, people would be saved (Bible, Genesis 3:14-15; Isaiah 53). In fact, the Bible says that 'it pleased the LORD' to offer Christ as a sacrifice for man's sin (Bible, Isaiah 53:10).

A judge sat in the courtroom, wearing his judicial robe. A young girl stood before him. She had been charged with driving without a licence and speeding down the motorway. The penalty for these charges was two thousand pounds. He pointed his finger at her and asked, 'Are you guilty or not?' to which she answered, 'Yes. Your Honour, *but I cannot afford to pay the penalty.'* The judge simply said, 'You *must* pay,' and then closed court. He stepped down from the bench, took off his robe and gave the girl two thousand pounds. Why? Because he was her father. He could not dishonour his name by letting her go free, but he was also merciful and loving and could not bear to see her put in jail because of her inability to pay. The only solution, therefore, was for him to pay the penalty himself.

In the same way, Christ has paid the penalty for our sin. God is holy. He hates sin, so he cannot simply close his eyes to our disobedience. Because he is a just and fair God, he must punish sinners. Death is our penalty; spiritual death, physical death, then ultimately, eternal separation from God. No mere man could ever pay that penalty for us. But in his mercy, God decided to pay the penalty himself so that we can go free. Jesus Christ, being equal with God, took off his robe of heavenly glory and came down to earth as a man. On the cross, he was punished for our sins. The justice and mercy of God came together, and both were satisfied. This is the sense in which he paid our debt. Without Jesus' death there would have been *no way* for us to escape God's punishment for our sin.

> On the cross, [Jesus] was punished for our sins. The justice and mercy of God came together, and both were satisfied.

Yet Jesus did more than just paying sinners' debts. His love is far greater than anyone can imagine. Let me explain by telling you the story of two brothers. As they grew older one of them got into a lot of debt and eventually became bankrupt. The other brother, by contrast, became very rich — a multimillionaire. When the rich one heard of his brother's problem through a friend, out of love he said to his brother, 'Why didn't you come to me for help yourself? Don't worry! I'll pay all your debts. They'll all be cancelled out.' So he did. He paid his brother's debt in full. What kindness and love! But what about exchanging their accounts? What if we were to ask the rich man to give all his possessions to his brother? 'Aha,' the rich brother might say, 'that's not possible. I cannot do any more than simply pay my brother's debt.'

Yet listen to what Jesus has done. As a follower of Jesus, he not only paid my debt, but he also gave me all his riches. A marvellous exchange took place, in which my sins were put to his account; in this way he paid my debt. But his goodness, his perfect life, were also put to my account so that, in God's sight, I am as righteous as Jesus Christ himself!

Oh, how great is the love of God! How greatly Jesus must have loved me to not only pay my debt but also give me his own goodness!

What is the evidence that Jesus' death was sufficient for man's salvation?

The evidence is the resurrection of Jesus from the dead. By raising Jesus from the dead, God declared to the world that he had accepted Jesus' sacrifice on our behalf.

If Jesus had remained in the grave, we would have seen that he was just another sinful human being like us. His death would have been worthless. He would have died for his own sins, not ours. As the Bible states, without the resurrection, we would have no hope, 'And if Christ is not risen, your faith is futile; you are still in your sins!' (Bible, 1 Corinthians 15:17).

The resurrection shows that death could not keep its hold on Jesus. It shows that God, the Judge, considered our penalty to have been paid. Our sins had been dealt with. Jesus broke the death barrier.

Anyone who has said goodbye to a departed loved one at a graveside knows that death is a formidable enemy. Yet, for Christians facing death, there is the certainty of eternal life beyond the grave. This certainty comes from the knowledge that Jesus Christ overcame death and its sting, which he accomplished through his triumphant resurrection. 'Death is swallowed up in victory. O Death, where is your sting?' (1 Corinthians 15:54-55).

If Jesus died on the cross, and if Jesus is God, does that mean that God died on the cross?

God is Spirit. In the original Hebrew language, Spirit is *roh*. From this word, the word *rihe* is taken, which means 'the air'. We can say, therefore, that God's Spirit is like the air in the atmosphere. Air is everywhere. Though you cannot see it, you know it is present: you can feel it, you breathe it, even though it has no colour or shape. Similarly, the Spirit of God is present everywhere.

An empty bottle does not contain any liquid, but you know that it is full of air. The air inside the bottle has taken the shape of the bottle, even though air has no shape. The characteristics of the air inside the bottle are similar to the characteristics of the air outside the bottle. The fact that there is air inside the bottle does not mean that there is no air outside the bottle! Now, if you were to take the bottle and smash it against a wall, it would break into hundreds of pieces. It would be shattered. Could we say that the air inside the bottle would also be shattered? No. Only the form that contained the air would have been shattered.

A similar thing took place when God, who is Spirit, dwelt among us in the person of Jesus Christ. God took the likeness of man. That did not mean that he existed no more. Rather, like the air when it filled the bottle, God still existed everywhere. Furthermore, Jesus' crucifixion did not mean that God was killed, but rather that the man Jesus died. God existed always, even during the three days in which Jesus was dead in the tomb.

I am so bad. God could never be interested in me!

When we look up at the stars and consider how vast the universe is we realize, to a small degree, how great God is. And we ask, 'Can the Great God, who made and sustains millions of stars, ever look at someone as small as I am? How could he care for me or hear my prayers? Surely God is too great to be interested in the affairs of individuals among the billions of people on this earth?'

Let us consider how Jesus treated individual people. Was he too great to be concerned about the joys and sorrows of ordinary people? By no means! On the contrary, we see that Jesus Christ had love and sympathy for every person he met. He wanted to give health and happiness and salvation to each one. Thousands of people came to Jesus for help: rich and poor, old and young, men and women, his own people and foreigners … no one was turned away. For Jesus said, 'The one who comes to Me I will by no means cast out' (Bible, John 6:37).

Jesus the friend of sinners!

We have all sinned against God. God could have destroyed us. But when we become acquainted with Jesus, the perfect manifestation of God, we are surprised to see that he does not hate sinners. Instead of condemning or avoiding them, Jesus often ate in their homes and showed them great kindness. For this strange conduct he was severely criticized by the religious leaders of the people, who called him 'a friend of sinners' (Bible, Luke 7:34 and 15:2). Jesus replied that these sinners were sick, and he was their physician. As the doctor does not wish to kill his patient but to make him well, so God does not want sinners to perish but to be saved. He came to seek and to save those who had lost their way and were dying in their sin.

> [Jesus] came to seek and to save those who had lost their way and were dying in their sin.

Can Jesus have time for a sinner like me?

In case you still doubt whether God is interested in you, let me tell you about the first people Jesus appeared to after he rose from the dead.

The first person who saw the risen Jesus was a nobody! Her name was Mary Magdalene. She had once been demon-possessed. Presumably she had lived the worst sort of life as a result. She was a nobody, but Jesus met her. Why? Because *Jesus has time for nobodies.*

Later that day Jesus appeared to a failure. One of his disciples had denied him three times in one night although he had said he would not. Jesus forgave this sorrowful man because *Jesus Christ has time for failures.*

On the same day he appeared to people who were confused. They were walking, and they could not understand the events which had happened in the previous few days. How could Jesus have been crucified? They had loved him so much. They had heard reports that he had been raised from the dead and they were perplexed. Then Jesus walked with them, because *he has time for people who are confused.*

There were also ten disciples who were so afraid that they locked the doors. Jesus did not unlock the doors. He just went in and stood where they were. Why did he meet them? Because *he has time for fearful people too.*

Then, there was one disciple who could not believe that Jesus had been raised from the dead. How did Jesus react to his doubts? Did he condemn the man? No! He went to meet him, because *Jesus Christ has time for doubters!*

Then there was a cynic, a man who had lived in the same house as Jesus in Nazareth, his half brother James. Throughout all those years he had not believed a word of what Jesus had said. His only comment on the situation had been that Jesus was mad. Yet Jesus met James and brought him to be a believer, because *Jesus has time for cynics!*

There was also one man who met Jesus a little later. He was a great opponent to Christianity, seeking to imprison and kill Christians. Do you know how Jesus treated him? As this man Saul was going on a death mission to Damascus to kill as many Christians as possible, Jesus met him in the middle of his sin! He said, 'Saul, Saul, why are you persecuting Me?'(Bible, Acts 9:4). Saul was converted, because *Jesus Christ even has time for his opponents.*

And so to the question: 'Does God care for individuals?' We confidently reply, 'Yes, he does! Look at Jesus Christ who is the image and revelation of the invisible God.' There is no class of people for whom Jesus Christ has no time. 'For God so loved the world that He gave His only begotten Son [Jesus], that whoever *[and you can put your name right here, right now]* believes in Him should not perish but have everlasting life' (Bible, John 3:16).

A personal invitation

Jesus is Lord!

Christians worship Jesus Christ not because he is a prophet, but because from eternity past he was the Word of God, the Son of God, perfectly one with God. He is not just an exalted man. Rather, he always was God, and he became man to save sinful people and restore their relationship with their Creator. Hence, he is worthy of worship.

If you are not a committed follower of Jesus, let me ask you a question: What do you think about Jesus Christ? Can you honestly say that he is merely another prophet or a great teacher? If you weigh the evidence, can you conclude that he was not God? I pray that God, who loves the world so much, will help you to see this issue very clearly. God wants us to turn away from our sin and to seek his mercy and forgiveness. 'Return to the LORD, and He will have mercy … and to our God, for He will abundantly pardon' (Bible, Isaiah 55:7). He wants to help people and set them free from the bondage of sin. His desire is that you will also be saved from its consequences. God is so concerned that he came to earth, taking the form of a man, so that you may know him personally, intimately and be reconciled to him. Will you receive him? What else could God ever have done for you?

Jesus is unlike any other. He invites you to come and follow him. He is offering you help for today and hope for tomorrow. His invitation will not be open for ever; but it is open for you now. Won't you say, 'YES'?

If you want to know and follow Jesus then simply tell him so. You can receive him into your life now by talking to him sincerely in prayer. Open your heart to him, acknowledge and confess your sins. Ask God to wash you from your sins by the blood that Jesus spilt on the cross. God forgives those who humble themselves before him in this way. He is perfectly aware of all that is in your heart, so it is useless trying to hide anything. Acknowledge God's right to reign in your life. Ask him to make you into the person he wants you to be.

I encourage you to take God's Holy Word (the Bible) very seriously. Don't let anything stop you putting right your relationship with God.

You may like to pray something like this:

Dear God, I confess I am a sinner. Thank you that Jesus took my punishment upon himself when he died on the cross for my sins, and then rose from the dead, defeating death. Today, I repent and place my trust in Jesus Christ alone for my salvation. In Jesus' name I pray. Amen.

If you have understood who Jesus is and prayed this prayer sincerely, then God will adopt you as his child and welcome you into his family. He will transform your life. The Bible promises, 'as many as received Him [Jesus Christ], to them He gave the right to become children of God, to those who believe in His name' (Bible, John 1:12).

Appendix 1

Answering the most common objections to the deity of Christ

During one of the apostle Paul's journeys, he travelled to the city of Berea. While he was there, he preached the way of salvation through Jesus Christ. His hearers there responded in a unique way. Whereas in some places people quickly reacted strongly against Paul's teaching, the Bereans were 'fair-minded'. They 'searched the Scriptures daily to find out whether these things *[what Paul said]* were so' (Bible, Acts 17:11).

However, in spite of the scriptural evidence supporting Jesus' deity, some continue to remain in denial simply because they have been indoctrinated to believe otherwise. Some Jehovah's Witnesses, Mormons and Muslims are like this. In order to refute what the Bible teaches and to justify their erroneous positions, they incorrectly isolate specific verses in the Bible,[1] quote only half verses, or take certain verses within a passage out of context.

The importance of context

For example, in John 14:28, Jesus said, 'My Father is greater than I.' This clause is often cited out of context — renewing the controversy from the early centuries that is connected with the name Arius.

The problem is knowing how to bring together two strands of John's (and the New Testament's) witness: one places Jesus on a level with God (John 1:1,18; 5:16-18; 10:30; 20:28); the other emphatically insists upon Jesus' obedience to his Father and on his dependence upon his Father (John 4:34; 5:19-30; 8:29; 12:48-49). It cannot be right to minimize the truth of one strand by appeal to the other. Arians emphasize the latter strand to deny the former: Jesus is less than fully God. Gnostics emphasize the former and underrate the latter: Jesus may in some sense be divine, but he is not fully human.

In each passage the immediate context resolves most of the difficulties. Here, 'My Father is greater than I' cannot mean that Jesus is a lesser god — that would not make sense in the context of Jewish monotheism. And neither can it mean that Jesus is not God. If I were to say to you, 'Her Majesty Queen Elizabeth II is greater than I', no one would take this to mean that she is more human than I am. The Queen is greater than I in wealth, authority, majesty, influence, renown — and doubtless in many other ways; only the surrounding discussion would clarify just what type of greatness was in view.

The relationship between the Father and the Son of God

In order to understand the quoted verses, one needs to grasp the sort of relationship that exists between the Son of God and the Father. That is the key issue.

The Son is God. He is not one-third of God, but fully God. What distinguishes the Son from the Father is not the divine nature of the Son. This is possessed equally and fully by the Father — and by the Holy Spirit too. What distinguishes the Son is his role in relation to the Father and to the Spirit, and the relationship that he has with each of them. Let's think about his relationship with the Father in detail.

The eternal generation of the Son

God has revealed himself to us as a Trinity of persons. The first of these persons is revealed as the Father, the second as the Son. But we must be careful not to think of their relationship in purely human terms. The pattern for human fatherhood derives from God the Father, not the other way around.

The relationship between the Son and the Father is unique. The Son is the eternal Son of the eternal Father. The Son is what he is because of the Father. The Scriptures often call Jesus 'the only begotten'. He is the 'only begotten

Son' (John 1:18; 3:16); 'the only begotten of the Father' (John 1:14); and 'the only begotten Son of God' (John 3:18). The Son owes his generation to the Father, not the Father to the Son. On other occasions the Son is called 'the image of the invisible God' (Colossians 1:15) and 'the express image' of God the Father (Hebrews 1:3). The Son could not be what he is without God the Father. But the Father, on the other hand, could not find expression without God the Son.

We must be very clear what we are saying here:

God the Father did not have a wife or mistress, as if he was like the pagan deities. Neither of the testaments speaks of God having sexual characteristics. In any case, 'God is Spirit' (John 4:24).

The Father did not create the Son. We have already seen that Jesus is totally God. He is God in the same sense as the Father is God and the Holy Spirit is God. Christians rejoice to sing a Christmas song based on the old Nicene Creed: 'I believe ... in one Lord Jesus Christ, the only-begotten Son of God, begotten of the Father before all worlds; God of God, light of light, very God of very God; begotten, not made, being of one substance with the Father, by whom all things were made.'

The Father did not make the Son God. Jesus is God in his own right. There was never a time when the Father suddenly decided to beget his Son. We are talking about a natural and eternal relationship in the Godhead. Louis Berkhof, a theologian, wrote, 'The generation of the Son must be regarded as a necessary and perfectly natural act of God. This does not mean that it is not related to the Father's will in any sense of the word. It is an act of the Father's necessary will *[i.e. it had to happen; it was not optional]*, which merely means that his concomitant will takes perfect delight in it *[he rejoices in it]*.'[2] Of course we cannot fully understand this with our limited human faculties.

The eternal generation of the Son does not make him less than God. In John 5:16-47, Jesus speaks both of his eternal generation and of his equality with God. This is one of the passages in Scripture that is beyond our understanding! On the one hand, he speaks of his eternal Sonship and how the Father had sent him. On the other hand, incomprehensibly to us, he asserts his divinity.

We have already touched on verses 17 and 18 of this chapter, and have seen how Jesus claims to be God by saying he is equal with his Father. Yet he goes on to say that he could not work independently. He could only judge because the Father had committed judgement to him (v. 22). However this does not mean that the Son is inferior to the Father, or that he should be treated with less honour than the Father. Verse 23 tells us that, 'All should honour the Son just as they honour the Father.'

Even though the Son does nothing independently from the Father, he is himself God in his own right.

The relationship between the Father and the Son did not have a beginning. We have already said that the relation between God the Son and God the Father must not be understood in human terms. In human relationships, a father exists before his son. This is not true when speaking of the first and second persons of the Trinity. The generation of the Son did not take place in time. Christ has *always* been the Son of God — not only from the time of his birth as a man. The second person of the triune Godhead has eternally existed as the Son. There was never a time when he was not the Son of God; and there has always been a Father–Son relationship within the Godhead. The Sonship is not merely a title or role that Christ assumed at some specific point in history; it is his essential identity as the second person of the Godhead.

There is considerable biblical evidence to support the eternal Sonship of Christ:

- Hebrews 13:8 teaches that 'Jesus Christ is the same yesterday, today, and for ever'; that is, Jesus' divine nature never changes. This indicates that he was always the Son of God because that is an essential part of his person. At the incarnation Jesus Christ became a man, but his divine nature did not change, nor did his relationship with the Father.
- This same truth is also implied in John 20:31, where we see John's purpose in writing his Gospel. He says that he wrote it 'that you may believe that Jesus is the Christ,

the Son of God, and that believing you may have life in His name'. It does not say that he *became* the Son of God but that he *is* the Son of God. The fact that Jesus was and is the Son of God is an essential aspect of his being and a key factor in his work in redemption.

- John 1:14-18 makes it clear that when the Son became a man, people were able to see the only begotten of the Father — but he was *already* the only begotten. The Word did not become God's Son, but being God's Son, he 'became flesh'.

- Other passages speak in the same way. He was God's Son before he was born (Romans 1:3; and Galatians 4:4). He was the Son of God before he came in the 'likeness of sinful flesh' (Romans 8:3). He was the Son of God before God sent him into the world (John 3:16; 1 John 4:9).

- Colossians 1:13-16 and Hebrews 1:2 clearly state that it was 'the Son' who created all things, thereby strongly implying that Christ was the Son of God at the time of creation. It was not a status which came later.

The Son's submission to the Father

One of the key aspects of the earthly life, work, ministry and mission of the Son is that he sought to do the will of the Father in everything. The Son's submission to the headship and authority of his Father must be carefully considered if we are to understand how the Father and Son relate to each other.

The head of Christ is God

In 1 Corinthians 11:3 Paul writes, 'But I want you to know that the head of every man is Christ, the head of woman is man, and the head of Christ is God.' Without doubt, the Son is under the authority, or headship, of the Father. Here Paul describes the authority and submission that occur in human relationships as a reflection of the authority and submission that exist in the eternal Godhead. God (the Father) is the head of Christ.

'But if Jesus Christ has a head', someone might say, 'then he can't be God. Doesn't this show that Jesus is inferior to the Father by nature?' If you argue in this way then, to be consistent, you would also have to say that a married woman is inferior to her husband — or even that she is not a human! But though a wife is subject to her husband in the Lord, she is *not* inferior to him by nature. The same is true of the relationship between the Lord Jesus and the Father.

There is a structure of authority and submission in the Godhead by which the Father and the Son (and the Holy Spirit) are distinguished. God has eternally designed it that way. We shall look now in more detail at this: while the Son lived on this earth, in eternity past and in eternity to come.

The Son's submission during his incarnation

The Son perfectly submitted to the Father during his incarnation and earthly mission. The evidence is overwhelming.

John's Gospel is full of indications that Jesus is God (John 1:1,18; 5:16-18; 10:30; 20:28), yet at the same time it shows his submission to the Father (John 4:34; 5:19-30; 8:29; 12:48-50). Jesus often expressed his constant desire to obey his Father. You will recall the episode in John 4 where Jesus was speaking to a Samaritan woman. His disciples had gone to get food. When they came back they asked him if he wanted something to eat. But Jesus answered, 'I have food to eat of which you do not know ... My food *[my sustenance, what nourishes me, what drives me]* is to do the will of Him who sent Me, and to finish His work' (John 4:32,34).

Another glimpse of the passionate submission that Jesus showed to his Father is seen in John 8. Jesus said to some religious leaders, 'You are from beneath; I am from above. You are of this world; I am not of this world' (John 8:23). Jesus clearly established his pre-existence prior to the incarnation, and implied that he was, in his very nature, uncreated and divine. Given this emphasis on his intrinsic deity, the statements by Jesus that follow are quite astonishing. A little later, Jesus said, 'When you lift up the Son of Man, then you will know that I am He, and *that I do nothing of Myself; but as My Father taught Me, I speak these things. And He who sent Me is with Me. The Father has not left Me alone, for I always do those things that please Him,'* (John 8:28-29, italics added).

What can we learn from this? Though Jesus claimed to be God, he said he did and spoke nothing on his own authority. He spoke only what the Father taught, and did only what pleased the Father. How amazing! Jesus is God, but Jesus obeyed God.

Notice the level of Christ's submission. It is complete, comprehensive, all-inclusive, and absolute. In Philippians 2:5-8, we are told to follow the example of Christ, 'who, being in the form of God, did not consider it robbery to be equal with God, but made Himself of no reputation, taking the form of a bondservant, and coming in the likeness of men. And being found in appearance as a man, He humbled Himself and became obedient to the point of death, even the death of the cross'. Jesus always submitted and obeyed his Father. He never once sinned at any point throughout the whole of his earthly life. He went to the cross absolutely sinless, having done nothing but the will of his Father (see, for example, 2 Corinthians 5:21 and Hebrews 4:15).

The Son's submission in eternity past

What about Jesus' relationship to the Father prior to the incarnation? Did Jesus submit to the Father only during his incarnation?

In 1 Peter 1:20-21, Peter wrote, '[Christ] ... was foreordained before the foundation of the world, but was manifest in these last times for you who through Him believe in God, who raised Him from the dead and gave Him glory, so that your faith and hope are in God.' God the Father appointed his Son as the one who would bring everything into subjection, the one who would be given the name that is above every other name. His Son would be given glory through his suffering, death, resurrection and exaltation. But when did the Father choose his Son for this calling? Peter's answer is, 'before the foundation of the world'; that is, before creation. This requires an authority-submission relationship in the Godhead in eternity past.

John 3:16 says, 'For God so loved the world that He gave His only begotten Son'. While Galatians 4:4 states that, 'When the fullness of the time had come, God sent forth His Son, born of a woman, born under the law.' Christ did not become God's Son by being given; he was given as God's Son. He was sent out as God's Son.

The submission of the Son during the incarnation is but a reflection of the eternal relationship that he has always had with his Father. The Son has always sought to do the will of the Father.

This is how Augustine (a fourth-century theologian) expresses it: 'If however the reason why the Son is said to have been sent by the Father is simply that the one is the Father and the other the Son then there is nothing at all to stop us believing that *the Son is equal to the Father* and consubstantial and co-eternal, and yet that the Son is sent by the Father. *Not because one is greater and the other less, but because one is the Father and the other is the Son;* one is begetter, the other begotten; the first one is the one from whom the sent one is; the other is the one who is from the sender. For the Son is from the Father, not the Father from the Son. In the light of this we can now perceive that *the Son is not just said to have been sent because the Word became flesh, but that He was sent in order for the Word to become flesh,* and by His bodily presence to do all that was written. That is, *we should understand that it was not just the man who the Word became that was sent, but that the Word was sent to become man.* For He was *not sent in virtue of some disparity of power or substance or anything in Him that was not equal to the Father,* but in virtue of the Son being from the Father, not the Father being from the Son.'[3]

Augustine denies that the Son's submission to the Father means that he is inferior. He has no problem saying on the one hand that there is eternal equality between the Father and Son, and on the other hand that the Son is sent from the Father, with the task of doing the will of the Father.

Augustine also denies that the Son's subordination began at the incarnation. The sending of the Son occurred in eternity past in order that the eternal Word (Jesus Christ) might take on a human body and then carry on his role of doing his Father's will.

The Son's submission in eternity to come

After accomplishing the mission the Father sent him to do, the Son will still be in total submission to the Father in the ages to come.

In Revelation 5:1-13, John portrays the grand heavenly scene. 'And I saw in the right hand of Him who sat on the throne a scroll written inside and on the back, sealed with seven seals ... And no one in heaven or on the earth or under the earth was able to open the scroll, or to look at it ... And I looked, and behold, in the midst of the throne and of the four living creatures, and in the midst of the elders, stood a Lamb as though it had been slain ... Then He came and took the scroll out of the right hand of Him who sat on the throne ... And every creature which is in heaven and on the earth and under the earth and such as are in the sea, and all that are in them, I heard saying, "Blessing and honour and glory and power be to Him who sits on the throne, and to the Lamb, for ever and ever!"'

Both now and into the future, the Son (depicted here as the Lamb) is worshipped in heaven with him who is on the throne. He is given the most profound adoration. The Son and the Father are seen equally and fully as God. Yet the Son is shown to be under the authority of the Father as he approaches the throne and takes the scroll, representing God's eternal plan, from the right hand of the Father: not by violence, nor by fraud, but because of his merit and his worthiness. God the Father very willingly and justly hands the book to Christ, and Christ as readily and gladly takes it, for he delights to reveal and to do the will of his Father.

Let us now look at Paul's teaching in 1 Corinthians 15. Talking about the future reign of Christ over all, Paul says, 'Then comes the end, when He *[the Son of God]* delivers the kingdom to God the Father, when He puts an end to all rule and all authority and power. For He must reign till He has put all enemies under His feet. The last enemy that will be destroyed is death. For "He has put all things under His feet." But when He says "all things are put under Him", it is evident that He who put all things under Him is excepted. Now when all things are made subject to him, then the Son Himself will also be subject to Him who put all things under Him *[the Father]*, that God may be all in all' (1 Corinthians 15:24-28).

At the end of the world, the Son will rule over all creation, bringing everything into subjection under his feet, but only because the Father has given all things to the Son. And though all creation will be subject to him, he himself will be subject to the Father.

An eternal Father–Son relationship

So what shall we conclude?

The Son is the eternal Son of the eternal Father. What was seen over and over again in the incarnational mission of Jesus Christ was simply the manifestation of what is eternally true in the relationship between the Father and the Son. The Son is in eternal submission to the authority of the Father. Authority and submission reside eternally in the Father–Son relationship. But the unique feature of Jesus' relationship to his Father is that no sin corrupts this purest model of submission and authority.

However, this submission does not compromise the oneness between the Father and the Son in any way. Jesus is no less God than his Father.

The loving relationship between the Son and the Father

It is quite remarkable that, although he is fully God, Jesus refuses to do anything apart from the Father's will! We must understand that this submission is not forced, but willingly and joyfully given out of love. We must never separate the Son's submission to the Father and his love for the Father. If we do, we will be in danger of misunderstanding the Father–Son relationship.

We may ask: If the Son always submits to the Father, can there really be a loving relationship between them? How can one who is eternally under the authority of another genuinely love the one over him? And how can the one in authority genuinely love the one who submits to him?

We must not answer such questions from our point of view, relying on our own intuitions, but look to the

Scriptures. What is the motive for the Son's submission to his Father? What lies behind it? The answer is his deep and abounding love for his Father. Consider for instance what Jesus said in John 14:31: 'But that the world may know that I love the Father, and as the Father gave Me commandment, so I do.' Jesus does what his Father commands him to do so that the world may know that he loves the Father. His glad obedience is rooted in this deep and abounding love for his Father. If we were to ask Jesus, 'What is the proof that you love the Father?' he would say, 'You can see I love my Father because I gladly and perfectly obey him.' The Son's obedience is the expression of the reality of his self-giving love to his Father.

If we were to ask the Lord Jesus another question, 'How *much* do you love your Father?' his answer might be expressed using the words of Philippians 2:8: 'And being found in appearance as a man, He humbled Himself and became obedient to the point of death, even the death of the cross.' The demands that were made of the Son and the cost of his willingness to obey are beyond our human comprehension. But that is how much the Son loves the Father. It shows itself in costly obedience. This is true love.

And what about the Father's love for his Son? Jesus is the Father's 'beloved Son'. The Father adores the Son, both for who he is and for what he is doing. The Father focuses all attention on him. He glorifies him, and he always has. The Father's love for his Son is shown in the wisdom of his command and its blessing. The Son who would perfectly obey would be honoured. Jesus said to his disciples, 'As the

Father loved Me, I also have loved you; abide in My love. If you keep My commandments, you will abide in My love, just as I have kept My Father's commandments and *[precisely because of that]* abide in His love' (John 15:9-10).

Yes, the Father loves the Son and the Son loves the Father. But this love relationship would be empty without the Father's authority and the Son's submission. At the heart of the love relationship between the Son and the Father are the obedience of the Son to the Father and the authority of the Father over the Son. The Son loves the Father and shows his love by obeying the Father. The Father loves the Son with a fatherly love. His great desire is that the Son might have supreme glory over all. He is satisfied that in eternity we will give honour and glory and praise to the Lord Jesus Christ seated on the throne of heaven. It is leadership, but leadership in love.

Conclusion

I am amazed at how many people have a problem with a hierarchical structure of authority within the Godhead. It is because they have a worldly view of submission and authority based on what they've seen on earth, and they cannot fathom that same kind of hierarchy in God. Their problem is that they are recreating God after their own image and likeness.

Instead of trying to impose our earthly understanding of submission on God, we should try to understand how exactly God the Father is the head of Christ, and then redefine our human relationships based on that perfect model.

Isn't it remarkable that this authority-submission relationship has been eternally exercised within the Godhead? Because the Son eternally submits to the Father, it indicates that authority and submission are eternal realities. It stands to reason that when God created the world he fashioned it in a way that reflects these eternal realities. It makes sense, then, that a similar authority-submission structure is found in marriage.

Once you grasp the sort of relationship that exists between the Son of God and the Father, verses such as Mark 13:32; John 5:19; 14:28; 17:3; 20:17; and 1 Corinthians 11:3 will make sense. The Son is God. What distinguishes the Son from the Father is not the divine nature. That is possessed equally and fully by the Father and the Holy Spirit also. What distinguishes the Son is his submissive role as Son in relation to the Father, and the relationship that he has with him.

The assumption that Jesus is anyone less than the LORD himself limits and challenges God's plan of salvation and his saving grace for mankind. The beauty of the gospel of Jesus Christ and God's plan for mankind's salvation cannot be fully appreciated until one understands that our Saviour is not just a man or an angel, but is none other than our beloved creator, the LORD himself!

Appendix 2

Old Testament prophecies about the Messiah

48 major prophecies — *fulfilment in italics*

His human origins

Born of the seed of woman	Gen. 3:15	*Matt. 1:20; Gal. 4:4*
Seed of Abraham	Gen. 22:18	*Matt. 1:1; Gal. 3:1*
Son of Isaac	Gen. 21:12	*Luke 3:23,34; Matt. 1:2*
Son of Jacob	Numbers 24:17	*Luke 3:23,34; 1:33; Matt. 1:2*
From the tribe of Judah	Gen. 49:10; Micah 5:2	*Luke 3:23,33; Matt. 1:2; Heb. 7:14*
From the family line of Jesse	Isaiah 11:1,10	*Luke 3:23,32; Matt. 1:6*
From the house of David	Jeremiah 23:5	*1 Chronicles 17:11-14; Matt. 1:1; Mark 10:47-48; Luke 3:23,31; Acts 13:22-23; Rev. 22:16*

His birth

| Born of a virgin | Isaiah 7:14 | *Matt. 1:18,24,25; Luke 1:26-35* |
| Born at Bethlehem | Micah 5:2 | *Matt. 2:1,4-8; John 7:42; Luke 2:4-7* |

Presented with gifts	Psalm 72:10; Isaiah 60:6	*Matt. 2:1,11*
Herod will kill children	Jeremiah 31:15	*Matt. 2:16-18*

His divine nature

His pre-existence	Micah 5:2; Isaiah 9:6-7; Prov. 8:22-23	*John 1:1-2; 8:58; 17:5,24; Col. 1:17; Rev. 1:17*
He shall be called LORD	Psalm 110:1	*Matt. 22:43-45; Luke 2:11*

His ministry

He will crush the head of Satan	Gen. 3:15	*Heb. 2:14; 1 John 3:8*
He will be a Prophet	Deut. 18:18	*Matt. 21:11; John 6:14*
He will be a Priest	Psalm 110:4	*Hebrews 3:1; 5:5-6; 7:26-27*
He will be a Judge	Isaiah 11:4; 33:22	*John 5:30; 2 Tim. 4:1*
He will be a King	Psalm 2:6; Zech. 9:9; Jer. 23:5	*Matt. 27:37; 21:5; John 18:33-38*
He will have a special anointing of the Holy Spirit	Isaiah 11:2; 42:1; 61:1-2	*Matt. 3:16-17; 12:17-21; Luke 4:15-21,43; John 1:32*
His zeal for God will be great	Psalm 69:9	*John 2:15-17*
He will be preceded by a messenger	Isaiah 40:3; Malachi 3:1	*Matt. 3:1-3; 11:10; Luke 1:17; John 1:23*

His ministry will begin in Galilee	Isaiah 9:1	*Matt. 4:12-13,17*
His ministry will be one of miracles	Isaiah 35:5-6; 32:3-4	*Matt. 9:32-35; 11:4-6; Mark 7:32-35; John 5:5-9; 9:6-11; 11:43-44,47*
He will teach in parables	Psalm 78:2	*Matt. 13:34-35*
He will enter into the Temple	Malachi 3:1	*Matt. 21:12*
He will enter Jerusalem on a donkey	Zech. 9:9	*Matt. 21:6-11; Luke 19:35-37*
He will be a stumbling block to the Jews	Psalm 118:22; Isaiah 8:14; 28:16	*1 Peter 2:7; Romans 9:32-33*
He will be a light of the nations	Isaiah 49:6; 60:3	*Acts 13:47-48; 26:23; 28:28; Luke 2:30-32*

His death and resurrection

He will be betrayed by a friend	Ps. 41:9; 55:12-14	*Matt. 10:4; 26:49-50; John 13:21*
He will be sold for 30 pieces of silver	Zech. 11:12-13	*Matt. 26:15; 27:3-7*
He will be forsaken by his disciples	Zech. 13:7	*Matt. 26:31; Mark 14:27, 50*
He will be silent before his accusers	Isaiah 53:7	*Matt. 27:12-14; Luke 23:9; 1 Peter 2:22-25*
He will be wounded and bruised	Isaiah 50:6; 53:5; Zech. 13:6	*Matt. 26:67; 27:26; 1 Peter 2:24*

He will be mocked	Psalm 22:7-8; 69:8-13	*Matt. 27:29-31,39*
His hands and his feet will be pierced	Psalm 22:16; Zech. 12:10	*Luke 23:33; John 20:25*
He will be crucified with thieves	Isaiah 53:12	*Matt. 27:38; Mark 15:27-28; Luke 22:37*
He will pray for those who persecute him	Isaiah 53:12	*Luke 23:34*
He will be hated without a cause	Psalm 69:4	*John 15:25*
His garments will be parted and cast for lots	Psalm 22:18	*John 19:23-24*
He will suffer thirst	Psalm 69:21	*John 19:28*
He will give a forsaken cry	Psalm 22:1	*Matt. 27:46*
He will commit himself to God	Psalm 31:5	*Luke 23:46*
His bones will not be broken	Exodus 12:46; Psalm 34:20	*John 19:33,36*
There will be darkness over the land	Amos 8:9	*Matt. 27:45*
He will be buried in a rich man's tomb	Isaiah 53:9	*Matt. 27:57-60*
He will rise from the dead	Psalm 16:10; 30:3; 118:18	*Matt. 28:6; Luke 24:46; Acts 2:31; 13:35*
He will ascend into heaven	Psalm 68:18	*Acts 1:9; Ephesians 4:8*
He will sit at the right hand of God	Psalm 110:1	*Mark 16:19; Acts 2:34; Hebrews 1:3*

Notes

Chapter 1

1. Bertrand Russell, *Why I am not a Christian*, Simon & Schuster, New York, p.19.
2. *Let God be true*, Watchtower Bible and Tract Society, p.33.
3. *Make sure of all things*, Watchtower Bible and Tract Society, p.207.
4. 'Who was Jesus?' *Larry King Live*. First broadcast 24 December 2004, CNN, http://transcripts.cnn.com/TRANSCRIPTS/0412/24/lkl. 01.html.
5. Dalai Lama, 'The Karma of the Gospel', *Newsweek*, 27 March 2000.
6. Mahatma Gandhi, *Harijan* (6 March 1937):25.
7. Quoted by Mark Driscoll & Gerry Breshears, *Vintage Jesus*, p.15.
8. As above.

Chapter 2

1. The Hebrew verb behind 'take an oath' has the same meaning as the verb Paul uses ('confess').
2. A student of the apostle John.

Chapter 6

1. 2 Clement 1:1. It is available at: http://www.earlychristianwritings. com/text/2clement-roberts.html
2. These letters are available at: http://www.saintignatiuschurch. org/letters.html
3. These epistles have been divided into chapters and verses, similar to the Bible. These references are in parentheses.

4. This is available at : http://www.earlychristianwritings.com/text/polycarp-lightfoot.html

5. Dods, Marcus, transl. *The First Apology of Justin Martyr*. Tyler, TX: Scroll Publ., 1989., p.98. This book is out of print, but the same text is available in *The First and Second Apology of Justin Martyr*, translated by Leslie Barnard.

6. Dods, p.106.

7. Cetnar, William. *Questions for Jehovah's Witnesses,* Kunkleton, PA: by the author, 1987, p.61.

8. Tatian the Assyrian, 'Address of Tatian to the Greeks', Chapter 21, in Roberts and Donaldson, *The Ante-Nicene Fathers*, Vol. 1, 74.

9. Fremantle, Anne, ed. *A Treasury of Early Christianity*. New York: Viking Press, 1953, p.396.

10. *Ibid.*, p.338.

11. Bush, L. Russ, ed. *Classical Readings in Christian Apologetics A.D. 100-1800*. Grand Rapids: Academie Books, 1983, pp.91-95.

12. *Exhortation to the Heathen*, 1.

13. In his *Letters* 10. 96-97.

14. There is no Latin word for 'a', therefore the phrase could be 'as to a god' or 'as to God'.

15. http://ccat.sas.upenn.edu/jod/texts/pliny.html

16. Lucian, *The Death of Peregrine*, 1113, in *The Works of Lucian of Samosata*, transl. by H. W. Fowler and F. G. Fowler, 4 vols. (Oxford: Clarendon, 1949), vol. 4, as cited in Habermas, Gary R., *The Historical Jesus: ancient evidence for the life of Christ* (Joplin, MO: College Press Publishing Company), 1996.

Conclusion

1. *Mere Christianity*, New York: Macmillan, 1952, pp.40-41.

Appendix 1

1. The following verses are often cited: Numbers 23:19; John 5:19; 14:28; 17:3; 20:17; 1 Corinthians 11:3; Colossians 1:15; Revelation 3:14.

2. Louis Berkhof, *Systematic Theology*, Banner of Truth, 2000, p.93.

3. Augustine, *Trinity*, trans. Edmund Hill, vol. 5, *The Works of St Augustine* (Brooklyn: New City Press, 1991), IV.27.

Bibliography

Blanchard, John. *Meet the real Jesus*, 1989, Evangelical Press.

Brown, Charles J. *The divine glory of Christ*, 1982, The Banner of Truth Trust, Edinburgh, Scotland.

Habermas, Gary R. *The Historical Jesus: ancient evidence for the life of Christ*, 2008, College Press, USA.

Ollyot, Stuart. *Jesus is Both God and Man: What the Bible teaches about the person of Christ*, Evangelical Press.

RBC Ministries. *Jesus: Who is this man who says he's God?*, 2004, RBC Ministries, Michigan, USA.

Sproul, R. C. *Mighty Christ: touching glory*, 1995, Christian Focus Publications, Scotland.

If you would like to receive further information
or receive free Christian literature, please contact us.
If you wish to make further study of the Christian faith,
correspondence courses
in English, Arabic or French are available at:

M.E.C. Word of Hope Ministries
PO Box 24
Rochdale
OL16 3FB
England

www.word-of-hope.net
E-mail: contact@word-of-hope.net